A Dictionary of Human Instincts

A Dictionary of Human Instincts

Nils K. Oeijord and Mitch C. Bronston

Authors Choice Press

San Jose New York Lincoln Shanghai

A Dictionary of Human Instincts

Authors Choice Press
an imprint of iUniverse.com, Inc.

For information address:
iUniverse.com, Inc.
5220 S 16th, Ste. 200
Lincoln, NE 68512
www.iuniverse.com

ISBN: 0-595-19746-9

Printed in the United States of America

To Sydney and Hanne

INTRODUCTION

"Life never occurs in main effects."

Abbott

"Nothing but the heart can change the heart."

Carroll O'Connor

"You cannot hold back a good laugh any more than you can the tide. Both are forces of nature."

William Rotsler

"Imagination is more important than knowledge."

Albert Einstein

"Curiosity has its own reason for existing."

Albert Einstein

This dictionary is thorough, but not complete. It contains many pairs, triples, etc of synonymous entries. Therefore a particular instinct, or a particular minimal unit of behavior, may appear several times in the list

The entries are 1) a normal, ordinary instinct, 2) a normal variant of an instinct, 3) an abnormal instinct, 4) a certain aspect of an instinct, 5) a reflex ("little instinct"), 6) the learned/learning part of an instinct (but it's nevertheless an innately specified behavioral trait), 7) a group of instincts, 8) an unclassified genetic minimal unit of behavior, or 9) a non-instinctual innate element of behavior.

The list of normal and abnormal natural behavior is long, but it is important to note that just about all human activity can be explained by the five **primal instincts** 1) the reproduction instinct, 2) the self-preservation instinct, 3) the territorial instinct, 4) the social-hierarchy instinct, and 5) the ritual instinct.

Even though we clock up more unique experiences as we age, evidence amassed over the past seventy-five years suggests that the "genetic contribution" to mental achievement and emotional characteristics **increases** with age!!! Example: The (broad) heritability coefficient of IQ is about 0.4 (= 40 %) when measured in children, about 0.6 (= 60%) in adolescents, and about 0.8 (= 80%) in later maturity. More learning causes **more** genetic determinism!?

Even reflexes can learn, so, of course, all instincts are learning instincts (= instincts can learn). Moreover, instincts are situational. Can we quantify how well a particular instinct can learn? Yes. This problem was solved by Mitch Bronston. His solution is to use the (broad) heritability coefficient, but let the "environmental" part of the coefficient (= of the variance) quantify how well an instinct can learn. The **Bronston heritability coefficient** directly explains the paradoxes above. It tells us that a behavioral trait's genetically determined specific learning ability/capacity is **decreasing** with age. But, fortunately, this coefficient also tells us that the other parts of the total ability/capacity of a behavioral trait are **increasing,** so that the total ability/capacity is pretty **constant** with age.

Even if environmentalism was only *partly* **correct, the Bronston coefficient had to** *decrease* **with age. Clearly, the** *increasing* **Bronston coefficient for human behavioral traits** *proves* **that human behavior is instinctive, and is not created by chaotic and poverty-stricken environmental factors.** But remember: 1) all instincts are learning instincts, and 2) all instincts are situational. Obviously, human intelligence(s) and intellect(s) depend on our having **more** instincts, not fewer.

A

a, the-*a*-speech-sounds instinct (The *a* speech sounds are the minimal units of instinctual speech sounds that correspond roughly to the letter *a* of the alphabet)

aback, you-are-taken-aback instinct (if you are taken aback, you are so surprised or shocked that you have to pause for a moment and cannot think or do anything)

abandon, to-abandon-oneself-to-an-emotion instinct

abandon, to-do-something-with-abandon instinct

abandoned, an-abandoned-way-of-behaving instinct

abase, to-abase-oneself instinct

abashed, to-be-abashed instinct

abhor, to-abhor-something instinct

abhorrence, abhorrence-of-evil instinct

abide, you-can't-abide-something instinct

abject, to-be-abject instinct (remember: instincts are situational)

ablaze, people's-eyes(-or-faces)-are-ablaze instinct

abnegation, abnegation instinct

abnormal, abnormal instincts (e.g. phobias, philias, manias, perversities, mental disorders)

above, to-be-above(-doing)-something instinct

above, to-be-above-someone (be in a position of emotional authority over them) instinct

abrasive, to-be-abrasive instinct

abreaction, abreaction instinct

abrupt, to-be-abrupt instinct

absent-minded, to-be-absent-minded instinct (or genetic, but non-instinctual, behavior?)

absent, to-be-absent (they are not paying attention to something because they are thinking about something else) instinct

absenteeism, absenteeism instinct (yes, genetic behavior!)

1

absorbed, absorbed-concentration instinct

absorbs, something-absorbs-someone (it interests them very much and takes up a lot of their time) instinct

abstracted, to-be-abstracted instinct

abstract, abstract-intelligence instinct

abstract, abstract-problem-solving instinct

abstract, abstract-reasoning instinct

abstract, abstract-thinking instinct

abstraction, abstraction (forming abstract ideas and concepts) instinct

absurdity, a-feeling-of-absurdity instinct

abuse, abuse-of-someone (cruel and violent treatment of them) instinct

abusive, to-be-abusive (say or write rude, offensive, or unkind things) instinct

academic, to-be-academic (be interested in studying) instinct

acarophobia, acarophobia (fear of mites/small insects or animals) instincts

acceptance, acceptance instinct

acceptance, feeling-of-acceptance instinct

acclamation, acclamation instinct

accommodate, to-accommodate-someone instinct

acculturation, acculturation instinct

accusation, accusation instinct

accustomed, to-be-accustomed-to-something(-or-to-something-happening) instinct

acerbity, acerbity instinct

achieve, the-will-to-achieve instinct

achievement, need-for-achievement instinct

acquire, to-acquire-a-taste(-or-habit) instinct

acquisitive, to-be-acquisitive instinct

acrid, acrid-words-or-remarks instinct

acrophobia, acrophobia (dread of or in high places) instinct

act out, act-out-your-feelings-or-ideas instinct

acting, acting-on-the-spur-of-the-moment instinct

actions, to-fear-the-actions-of-strangers instinct

activity, activity instinct (general-activity instinct)

activity, the-level-of-activity instinct

actor/actress, actor/actress instinct

actualization, self-actualization instinct

acumen, acumen instinct

acumen, inferential-acumen instinct

adamant, to-be-adamant-about-something instinct

adaptability, adaptability-to-change instinct

addicted, to-be-addicted-to-something instinct

addled, to-be-addled (confused and unable to think properly) instinct (yes, genetic behavior!)

adhere, to-adhere-to-a-*particular*-opinion-or-belief instinct

admiration, admiration instinct

admiration, a-warm,-passionate-admiration-for-fine-deeds instinct

admiration, smiles-of-admiration instinct

admired, we-want-to-be-admired-by-others instinct

admonition, admonition instinct

adoration, adoration instinct

adoring, to-look-at-someone-in-a-loving-and-adoring-way instinct

adornment, adornment instinct

adornment, bodily-adornment instinct

adornment, the-adornment-of-females instinct

adulation, adulation (very great and uncritical admiration and praise) instinct (Hitler's Germany!)

adventure, to-enjoy-adventure instinct

adventure, to-seek-adventure instinct

advertisement, self-advertisement instinct

advertisement, sexual-advertisement instinct

advice, advice instinct

aesthetic, aesthetic-pleasure instinct

aesthetic, aesthetic-talking instinct

aesthetic, the-desire-for-aesthetic-expression instinct
affectation, affectation instinct
affection, affection-and-sense-of-mercy-towards-others instinct
affection, a-need-for-affection instinct
affection, seeking-affection instinct
affectionate, to-be-affectionate instinct
affective, affective-fixation instinct
affiliation, the-need-for-affiliation instinct
aflame, someone's-face-is-aflame instinct
afraid, to-be-afraid instinct
after, after-dinner-nap instinct
afterthought, afterthought instinct
against, to-be-against-someone instinct
against, to-do-something-against-someone-or-something instinct
agape, to-be-agape (your mouth is open, because you are very surprised by something) instinct
aggression, aggression-between-rival-females instinct
aggression, aggression-between-rival-males instinct
aggression, aggression-induced-by-a-desire-to-control-others instinct
aggression, aggression-induced-by-a-desire-to-push-forward-one's-own-ideas-or-interests instinct
aggression, anger-induced-aggression instinct
aggression, counter-attack-aggression instinct
aggression, displaced-aggression instinct
aggression, fear-induced-aggression instinct
aggression, frustration-induced-aggression instinct
aggression, hostile-aggression (where the sole aim is to harm another) instinct
aggression, impulsive-aggression instinct
aggression, instrumental-aggression instinct
aggression, interfemale-aggression instinct
aggression, intermale-aggression instinct

aggression, irritable-aggression instinct
aggression, moralistic-and-disciplinary-aggression instinct
aggression, parental-aggression (protects the young) instinct
aggression, people-who-are-frustrated-react-with-anger-and-aggres-sion instinct
aggression, predatory-aggression instinct
aggression, sadistic-aggression instinct
aggression, sexual-aggression instinct
aggression, stress-induced-aggression instinct
aggression, territorial-aggression instinct
aggression, the-baby's-aggression instinct
aggression, verbal-aggression instinct
aggression, violent-aggression instinct
aggression, wanton-aggression instinct
aggression, weaning-aggression instinct
aggressive, aggressive-intention-movements instinct
aggressive, aggressive-redirection-activity (e.g. a wife smashes a vase to the floor) instinct
aggressive, aggressive-responses-to-members-of-rival-groups instinct
aggressive, aggressive-sweating instinct
aggressive, scaling-of-responses-in-aggressive-interactions instinct
aggressiveness, aggressiveness instinct
aggrieved, to-be-aggrieved instinct
aghast, to-be-aghast (filled with horror and surprise) instinct
agitated, to-be-agitated instinct
agitation, agitation instinct
agnosticism, agnosticism instinct
agog, to-be-agog instinct
agonize, to-agonize-over-something instinct
agonized, the-agonized-grimace instinct
agonized, to-be-agonized (showing by what you say or do that you are in great pain, either physically or mentally) instinct

agony, to-scream-in-agony instinct

agony, you-are-in-agony (or in agonies) instinct

agony, you-are-piling-on-the-agony instinct

agoraphobia, agoraphobia (dread-in,-and-of,-open-spaces) instinct

agreeableness, agreeableness instinct

a-ha, a-ha-experience instinct

aha, 'Aha!'-response-involving-an-up-and-back-tilt-of-the-head instinct

aichmophobia, aichmophobia (fear of pointed instruments) instinct

ailurophobia, ailurophobia (fear of cats) instinct

aim, the-human-urge-to-aim-at-something instinct (there are more aiming sports today than all other forms of sport together)

airs, someone's-airs-and-graces instinct (they behave in a way that shows that they think that they are more important than other people)

alacrity, alacrity instinct

alarm, an-alarm-cry(or scream)-in-moments-of-fleeing-or-panic instinct

alarmed, to-become-alarmed-or-frightened instinct

alert, the-sound-of-rustling-leaves-is-enough-to-alert-us-when-we-are-walking-in-the-woods instinct

alertness, alertness instinct

algophobia, algophobia (abnormal fear of pain) instinct

alienation, alienation (a-feeling-of-strangeness-or-separation-from-others) instinct

alignment, alignment instinct

allegiance, allegiance instinct

alliances, making-alliances instinct

aloneness, feeling-of-aloneness instinct

aloud, fear-of-speaking-aloud instinct

altruism, heightened-altruism-toward-closest-kin instinct

altruism, reciprocal-altruism instinct

altruistic, altruistic-behavior-toward-non-relatives instinct

amathophobia, amathophobia (fear of dust) instinct

amaxophobia, amaxophobia (fear of riding in a vehicle) instinct amazement, amazement instinct

ambiguity, tolerance-of-ambiguity instinct

ambition, ambition instinct

ambition, competitive-ambition instinct

ambivalence, ambivalence instinct

amble, to-amble (walk slowly and in a relaxed manner) instinct

amiability, amiability (being friendly and pleasant) instinct

amok, amok (an acute, murderous frenzy) instinct (to-run-amok instinct)

amorous, amorous-feelings-and-behavior instinct

amuse, infants-amuse-themselves-and-their-families instinct

amuse, to-amuse-oneself-and-others instinct

amusement, amusement instinct (to-be-amused-by-something instinct)

anal, anal-eroticism instinct

analogical, analogical-reasoning instinct

analyze, to-analyze-something instinct

anathematization, anathematization instinct

androphobia, androphobia (fear of man (the species)/the male sex) instincts

anemophobia, anemophobia (fear of wind/air) instincts

anger, feelings-of-anger instinct

anger, gestures-of-anger instincts

anginophobia, anginophobia (fear of suffocation or being suffocated/fear of an attack of angina) instincts

angry, angry-crying instinct

angry, angry-outbursts instinct

angry, the-angry-face instinct

angry, to-be-angry-that-you-cannot-make-others-as-you-wish-them-to-be instinct

anguish, anguish instinct

animal, the-interest-in-the-animal-world instinct

animated, to-be-animated (lively and interesting) instinct

animosity, animosity (a feeling of strong dislike and anger) instinct

annoyance, annoyance instinct

answering, answering instinct

antagonism, antagonism (hatred or hostility) instinct

anthrophobia, anthrophobia (fear of man (singly)/society) instincts

anti, anti-contact-behavior instinct

anti, anti-stare instincts (covering the eyes with the hands, burying the face in the crook of the elbow, closing the eyes, etc)

anticipation, nervous-anticipation instinct

anticipation, the-feeling-of-anticipation instinct

antipathy, antipathy instinct

anxiety, anxiety-at-the-presence-of-strangers instinct

anxiety, the-feeling-of-anxiety instinct

anxiousness, anxiousness instinct

aphephobia, aphephobia (fear of being touched by another person) instinct

apiphobia, apiphobia (fear of bees) instinct

apologetically, apologetically-hug-and-kiss-the-child instinct

apology, to-make-an-apology instinct

appeased, to-be-appeased-by-submissive-gestures instinct

appeasement, a-sensation-of-appeasement instinct

appeasement, appeasement instinct (e.g. to appease the mountain)

appeasement, appeasement-signals instincts

appetite, appetite instinct

appetite, the-general-appetite-for-life instinct

applaud, to-applaud-someone-after-a-good-performance instinct (applause instinct)

apply, apply-your-mind-or-attention-to-something instinct

appreciation, appreciation instinct

apprehension, apprehension-span instinct

apprehensions, apprehensions (feelings of worry or fear about the future) instinct

approaches, to-play-with-novel-approaches instinct

approval, moral-approval instinct

approval, the-feelings-of-approval-and-disapproval instinct

approving, approving-gesture-or-expression instinct

aquaphobia, aquaphobia (fear of water/swimming) instincts

arachneophobia, arachneophobia (fear of spiders) instinct

arbitration, arbitration instinct

arch look, arch-look-or-expression (is mischievous or cunning) instinct

ardent, ardent-about-something instinct

argue, to-argue(-fiercely) instinct

arguments, to-like-to-pick-arguments instinct

arithmetic, arithmetic instinct

aroma, aroma instinct

arousal, arousal (the state of being alert or excited) instinct

arousal, emotional-arousal instincts

arousal, sexual-arousal instinct

arrogance, arrogance instinct

arrogate, you-arrogate-something instinct

art, art instinct

artistic, artistic-creation instinct

ascendance, ascendance instinct

asceticism, asceticism instinct

ashamed, to-feel-ashamed instinct

ashen, to-be-ashen instinct (someone who is ashen looks very pale because they are afraid or shocked)

ask, to-ask-someone-something instinct

asleep, falling-asleep instinct

asperity, asperity instinct (asperity is impatience and sternness that you express in your tone of voice)

aspiration, aspiration instinct

aspiration, the-thrill-of-aspiration instinct

assault, assault instinct

assault, assault-on-someone's-beliefs-or-attitudes instinct (also often an attempt to change them!)

assertion, assertion instinct

assertion, self-assertion instinct
assertive, to-be-assertive instinct
assertiveness, assertiveness instinct
assimilate, assimilate-new-ideas instinct
association, association instinct
association, free-association instinct
associative, associative inhibition instinct
assumption, to-make-an-assumption instinct
assurance, assurance (a feeling of confidence and lack of doubt) instinct
assurance, self-assurance instinct
astonishment, astonishment instinct
astound, something-or-someone-astounds-you instinct
astraphobia, astraphobia (fear of lightning/thunderstorms) instincts
astringent, astringent-behavior (behavior in which you criticize someone or something severely) instinct
at ease, feeling-at-ease-with-someone instinct
at ease, feeling-not-at-ease-with-someone instinct
'at-homeness', 'at-homeness' instinct
atheism, atheism instinct
athletic, an-interest-in-athletic-skills instinct
atonement, atonement instinct
atonement, a-gesture-of-atonement instinct
attachment, attachment-bond (e.g. between an infant and its mother) instincts
attack, attack-someone (use violence against them) instinct
attack, personal-attack instinct
attack, physical-attack instinct
attack, political-attack instinct
attack, verbal-attack instinct
attacker, the-attacker-suddenly-explodes-with-a-rapid-series-of-blows-and-kicks instinct
attention, attention instincts

attention, attention-getting-feat instinct
attention, attention-seeking instinct
attention, attention-span instinct
attention, selective-attention instinct
attention, something-catches-your-attention instinct
attention, to-focus-your-attention instinct
attention, to-summon-parental-attention instinct
attentiveness, attentiveness instinct
attraction, attraction (feeling of liking someone very much) instinct
attractive, dominance-in-a-man-is-considered-attractive-by-women instinct
attractive, tall-men-are-considered-more-attractive-by-women-than-short-men instinct
attractive, to-make-oneself-seem-attractive instinct
attractive, poise,-self-assurance,-optimism,-efficiency,-perseverence,-courage,-decisiveness,-intelligence,-and-ambition-are-things-women-find-attractive-in-a-man instinct
audacious, audacious-behavior instinct
audacity, audacity instinct
audition, audition instinct (audition=the sense of hearing)
auditory, auditory-imagery instinct
auditory, auditory-localization instinct
aunt, aunt-behavior instinct
authoritarian, to-be-authoritarian instinct (authoritarianism instinct)
authority, the-readiness-to-abandon-private-judgement-for-some-external-authority instinct
autoeroticism, autoeroticism instinct
autohypnosis, autohypnosis instinct
automatized, automatized-behavior (e.g. cardriving) instinct
autophobia, autophobia (fear of oneself/being alone) instincts
avenge, avenge-a-wrong-or-harmful-act instinct
avenging, avenging instinct
aversion, aversion instincts

aversive, any-aversive-event-may-trigger-off-violence instincts
avert, to-avert-one's-eyes-or-gaze-from-someone-or-something instinct
aviophobia, aviophobia (fear of flying) instinct
avoidance, avoidance instincts
avoiding, avoiding-pain instinct
avowed, you-are-an-avowed-believer-in-something instinct
awareness, a-conscious-perceptual-awareness-of-the-thing-that-is-impor-tant-right-then-and-an-unawareness-of-things-that-are-not-important instinct
awareness, awareness-of-other-people's-feelings instinct
awareness, conscious-awareness instinct
awareness, unconscious-awareness instinct
awareness, unconscious-awareness skills instincts
awareness, visual-awareness instinct
awe, awe instinct
awkwardness, feelings-of-awkwardness instinct (instincts are situational!)

B

b, the-*b*-speech-sounds instinct (The *b* speech sounds are the minimal units of instinctual speech sounds that correspond roughly to the letter *b* of the alphabet)
babble, idle-babble instinct
babble, to-babble instinct
babies, babies-babble instinct
babies, male-babies-like-male-babies-better-than-female-babies,-but-female-babies-do-not-show-any-preference-for-either-sex instincts
baby, the-baby-can-swim instinct
babyface, the-babyface-signal-release-protective-feelings instinct
baby's, baby's-general-smile instinct
baby's, baby's-parental-recognition-gurgle instinct
baby's, baby's-reflex-smile instinct

baby's, baby's-specific-smile instinct

baby's-sucking instinct

baby's-weeping instinct

baby talk, baby-talk instinct (the baby talk that adults use with infants may help them learn to speak)

bacillophobia, bacillophobia (fear of bacilli (germs)) instinct

back-away, to-back-away-from-someone-or-something (walk slowly backwards and away from them because you are frightened or nervous) instinct

backbiting, backbiting instinct

backs, backs-to-the-wall instinct (no one ever voluntarily selects a center table in an open space)

bad-tasting, bad-tasting-food instincts

bad-tempered, to-be-bad-tempered instinct

badger, to-badger-someone instinct

bafflement, bafflement instinct

bah, to-say-'bah'-in-order-to-express-scorn,-disappointment,-or-irritation instinct

balance, balance instinct

balky, the-balky-age instinct

ballistophobia, ballistophobia (fear of thrown objects/missiles) instinct

bandinage, bandinage instinct

banging, banging-things instinct (both chimps and children like banging things)

banter, banter (teasing or joking talk that is amusing and friendly) instinct

barbarism, barbarism instinct

bare, people-bare-their-teeth-when-enraged instinct

baresthesia (the sense of pressure and weight), the-emotional-aspects-of-baresthesia instinct

barracking, barracking instinct

barrage, a-barrage-of-questions,-complaints,-criticisms,-etc instinct

bashfulness, bashfulness instinct

basiphobia, basiphobia (fear of walking/standing erect and walking) instincts

bated breath, to-wait-for-something-with-bated-breath instinct

bathing, bathing instinct

bathophobia, bathophobia (dread of depths) instinct

bathyesthesia, bathyesthesia (deep sensitivity), the-emotional-aspects-of-bathyesthesia instinct

baton signals, baton-signals instinct

batter, to-batter-someone instinct

battle, battle-cry instinct

battle, the-cheer-excitement-of-battle instinct

bawl, to-bawl instinct

beaming, a-beaming-smile instinct

bear, bear-hug instinct

beasts of prey, to-fear-beasts-of-prey instinct

beat, 'It-beats-me' instinct

beat time, the-speaker-beat-time-to-his-words-with-small-head-jerks-or-hand-movements instinct

beat time, to-beat-time-to-a-piece-of-music instinct

beat up, to-beat-up-someone instinct

beautiful, beautiful-women-smell-nice instinct

beauty, appreciation-of-beauty instinct

beauty, universal-aspects-of-beauty instincts

beckoning, beckoning instinct

bedroom, make-bedroom-eyes-at-someone instinct

begging, begging instinct (apes and dogs beg!)

begging, begging-or-pleading-gesture:-palms-turned-upwards instinct

begging, the-begging-or-imploring-posture instinct

begrudge, to-begrudge-someone-something instinct

beholden, to-be-beholden-to-someone instinct

belief, belief (a feeling of certainty that something exists or is good) instinct

belief, belief-perseverance instinct

belittle, to-belittle-someone-or-something instinct
belligerence, belligerence instinct
bellowing, bellowing instinct
belly, belly-laugh instinct
belonephobia, belonephobia (fear of sharp, pointed objects) instinct
belongingness, the-need-for-belongingness-and-love instinct
bemoaning, bemoaning instinct
benevolence, benevolence instinct
berating, berating instinct
bereavement, bereavement instinct
berserk, to-go-berserk instinct
beseeching, beseeching instinct
beside yourself, to-be-beside-yourself-with-a-particular-feeling-or-emotion instinct
besmirching, besmirching instinct
besotted, to-be-besotted-with-someone-or-something instinct
bestiality, bestiality instinct
betrayal, fear-of-betrayal instinct
bewail, to-bewail-something instinct
bewilderment, bewilderment instinct
bewitched, to-be-bewitched instinct
bias, bias instinct
bibliophobia, bibliophobia (fear of books/irrational *hatred* of books) instincts
bickering, bickering instinct
big-hearted, to-be-big-hearted instinct
bigotry, bigotry instinct
biofeedback, biofeedback instincts
biological, biological-clocks instincts
biological, biological-intuition instinct
biological, biological-rhythms instincts

biophilia, biophilia instinct (the secure biophilic pleasure from the
nearness of animals and growing plants)
    birds, "birds of a feather flock together" instinct
    birds of prey, children-fear-birds-of-prey instinct
    birth, birth-cry instinct
    bisexuality, bisexuality instincts
    bitching, bitching instinct
    biting, biting instinct (there is perhaps a slight sex difference here)
    bitterness, bitterness instinct
    black-despair, to-feel-black-despair instinct
    black humor, black-humor instinct
    black mood, to-be-in-a-black-mood instinct
    blame, blame-avoidance-need instinct
    blame, to-blame instinct
    blame, to-blame-oneself instinct
    blame, to-try-to-avoid-blame instinct
    blank, your-mind-goes-blank instinct
    blase', to-be-blase' instinct
    blind obedience, blind-obedience instinct
    bliss, bliss instinct
    bliss, love-bliss instinct
    bloated, to-be-bloated-after-eating-a-meal instinct
    bloating gorges, bloating-gorges instinct
    blood, blood-and-injection-phobia instinct
    blood, dread-of-the-sight-of-blood instinct
    blood lust, blood-lust instinct
    bloodthirsty, to-be-bloodthirsty instinct
    blow, the-overarm-blow instinct
    blow, to-blow-your-nose instinct
    blows, to-come-to-blows instinct
    blue, to-feel-blue instinct
    bluffing, bluffing instinct

blunt, being-blunt instinct
blurt, to-blurt-out-something instinct
blush, blush instinct
bluster, bluster instinct
boast, boast instinct
bodily activity, bodily-activity instincts
body, the-brain-places-its-body instinct
body adornment, body-adornment instinct
body contact, body-contact (skin-contact) instinct
body contact, body-contact-tie-signs instincts (e.g. a hand on the shoulder is experienced as a sign of friendship, touching the adult head is experienced as condescending or sexual, touching the elbow emphasizes something)
body fragrance, after-only-forty-five-hours-the-newborn-can-tell-its-own-mother-from-other-mothers-purely-by-her-body-fragrance instinct
body language, body-language instincts
body privacy, body-privacy-and-contact-taboo instincts
body sag, body-sag-as-defeat-signal instinct
body senses, body-senses instincts
body shape, the-perception-of-desirable-body-shape instinct
body stress reactions, body-stress-reactions instincts
body stroking, body-stroking-and-caressing instincts
boldly, looking-boldly-head-on-at-someone instinct
boldness, boldness instinct
bonhomie, bonhomie instinct
boo, to-boo-someone instinct
boohoo, to-boohoo instinct
boost, to-boost-someone-or-something instinct
bored, to-be-bored instinct
boredom, reactions-to-boredom instincts
boredom, repetition-begets-boredom instinct
bosom, to-take-someone-to-your-bosom instinct
bossiness instinct

bottle up, bottle up, to-bottle-up-a-strong-emotion-that-you-feel instinct
bound, to-feel-bound-to-do-something instinct
bow down, to-bow-very-low-in-order-to-show-great-respect instinct
box, to-box-a-child's-ears instinct
boy or girl, children-have-a-stable-concept-of-what-it-means-to-be-a-boy-or-girl instinct
brace, to-brace-oneself instinct
brachiating, brachiating instinct
bragging, bragging instinct
brain, to-have-something-on-the-brain instinnct
brainstorm, brainstorm (a sudden insightful idea, usually accompanied by a compelling emotional reaction) instinct
bravado, bravado instinct
brave, to-be-brave instinct
bravely, to-fight-bravely instint
bravery, bravery instinct
bravery, bravery-on-the-field-of-battle instinct
bravura, bravura instinct
brawl, brawl instinct
breath, holding-my-breath,-not-daring-to-move instinct
breath, something-takes-your-breath-away instinct
breathless, breathless-suspense instinct
bridle, to-bridle instinct
brilliant, a-brilliant-smile instinct
brisk, to-be-brisk instinct
broadly, to-smile-broadly instinct
brontophobia, brontophobia (fear of thunder) instinct
brood, to-brood-about-something instinct
broody, to-get-broody-when-you-see-small-babies instinct
brow, sweating-brow instinct
brows, to-knit-one's-brows instinct
brush by, to-brush-by-someone instinct

brush off, to-brush-someone-off instinct

brusqueness, brusqueness instinct

brutality, brutality instinct

bubbling, bubbling-over-with-joy,-happiness,-etc instincts

bubbling, bubbling-with-a-good-feeling instinct

buffeted, you-are-buffeted-by-something instinct

buffoonery, buffoonery-makes-you-laugh instinct

bullied, people-who-look-confident-are-less-likely-to-be-bullied instinct

bullies, most-kids-fear-and-dislike-aggressive-bullies instinct

bullying, to-enjoy-bullying instinct (an individual may enjoy bullying, but think poorly of himself for acting in this way)

buoyancy, buoyancy instinct

burn, something-burns (it gives you a painful hot feeling) instinct

burning, burning-face-or-cheeks instinct

burning, to-be-burning-to-do-something instinct

burst in, to-burst-in-on-someone instinct

burst into, to-burst-into-laughter instinct

burst into, to-burst-into-tears instinct

burst out, to-burst-out-crying instinct

bury, to-bury-a-particular-feeling-of-something instinct

bury, to-bury-a-particular-memory-of-something instinct

bury, to-bury-your-face-in-your-hands instinct

bust-up, bust-up (serious quarrel which ends a relationship) instinct

busy, to-busy-yourself-with-something instinct

butchery, butchery instinct (the cruel killing of a lot of people/great apes)

butterflies, to-have-butterflies-in-one's-stomach instinct

bystander, bystander-effect instinct

C

c, the-*c*-speech-sounds instinct (The *c* speech sounds are the minimal units of instinctual speech sounds that correspond roughly to the letter *c* of the alphabet)

cackle, to-cackle (laugh in a loud unpleasant way) instinct

cainotophobia, cainotophobia (fear of novelty/new things/new ideas) instincts (also called cenotophobia)

call, to-call-someone-names (to insult someone by using offensive words) instinct

callousness, callousness instinct

calm, a-feeling-of-calm instinct

calm, a-sense-of-calm instinct

calm, you-calm-down intinct

camaraderie, camaraderie instinct

candidness, candidness instinct

candor, candor instinct

cannibalistic, cannibalistic-tendencies instinct (our closest relatives, chimpanzees, are not averse to eating their own, and research suggests cannibalism has a long history among humans)

canniness, canniness instinct

canny, a-canny-smile instinct

caper, caper (a light-hearted practical joke or trick) instinct

caper, to-caper instinct

caprice, caprice instinct

capriciousness, capriciousness instinct

captivate, someone-or-something-captivates-you instinct

cardiophobia, cardiophobia (fear of heart problems) instinct

care, care (a feeling of concern, anxiety, or worry about something) instinct

care, involvement-of-male-in-parental-care instinct

care, medical-care instinct

care, prolonged-maternal-care instinct
care, to-care-about-others instinct
carefulness, carefulness instinct
caressing, caressing instinct
careworn, to-look-careworn instinct
caring, caring (loving or affectionate behavior, or affectionate feelings) instinct
carnage, carnage instinct
carnal, carnal-desires/feelings instincts
carnival, carnival instinct
carsick, carsick instinct (yes, genetic behavior!)
castigation, castigation instinct
catcall, catcall instinct
catch, something-catches-your-attention instinct
catch, to-catch-oneself-doing-something instinct
categorization, categorization instinct
catharsis, catharsis (emotional release) instinct
catotrophobia, catotrophobia (fear of mirrors/breaking of a mirror) instincts
causality, innate-given-knowledge-of-causality instinct
cavil, to-cavil instinct (cavilling instinct)
cavorting, cavorting instinct
celebrate, celebrate, to-celebrate-lavishly-and-joyfully instinct
celebration, celebration instinct
celebration, victory-celebration instinct
cenotophobia, cenotophobia (fear of novelty/new things/new ideas) instinct (also called cainotophobia)
censure, censure (a strong disapproval and condemnation of something that has been done, or of the way it was done) instinct
censure, moral-censure instinct
ceremony, ceremony instinct
certainty, a-feeling-of-certainty instinct
certitude, certitude instinct

chagrin, chagrin instinct

challenge, to-like-a-challenge instinct (If skill is too little in relation to the task, people become anxious. But something easily achieved is boring. An experience where there is a balance between skill and the difficulty of a task evoked joy even if dangerous.)

chanting, chanting instinct

character, admiration-for-character instinct

charade, charade instinct

charismatic, charismatic-authority instinct

charity, charity-towards-strangers instinct

charm, charm instinct

charm, charm-offensive instinct

charm, to-charm-and-seduce-the-sex-object instinct

charming, finding-someone-to-be-charming instinct

charmingness, charmingness instinct

chary, to-be-chary instinct

chase, the-thrill-of-the-chase instinct

chasten, you-chasten-someone instinct

chastity, chastity instinct

chat, chat instinct

chatter, chatter instinct

chatter, feeling-the-need-to-keep-up-a-stream-of-cheerful-chatter instinct

chauvinism, chauvinism instinct

cheap, to-feel-cheap instinct

cheated, to-feel-cheated instinct

cheater, to-know-a-cheater-when-you-see-one instinct

cheating, catching-people-who-are-cheating-on-a-social-bargain instinct

cheating, cheating instinct

cheating, our-cheating-hearts instinct

cheer, to-cheer instinct

cheerful, cheerful-mood instinct

cheerfulness, cheerfulness instinct

chemical-sense, sense instincts
cherish, you-cherish-something
cherophobia, cherophobia (fear of fun/gaiety) instincts
chest, men-thrust-out-their-chest instinct (gorillas pound their chest)
chewing, chewing instinct
child-parent fixation, child-parent-fixation instinct
children, to-place-his/her-children-above-all-else instinct
chilly, you-feel-chilly instinct
chirp, to-chirp instinct
chivalry, chivalry instinct
choice, choice instinct
choice, feelings-of-choice instinct
choke, something-chokes-you instinct
choke, to-choke-back-a-strong-emotion instinct
choleric, to-be-choleric-with-rage instinct
chortle, to-chortle instinct
chortle, to-chortle-to-oneself instinct
christen, to-christen-someone-or-something instinct
chromaesthesia, chromaesthesia (to perceive sounds as colors) instinct
(colored hearing instinct)
chuckle, to-chuckle instinct
chuckles, loud-play-chuckles instinct
chunking, chunking instinct (chunking is the organization process
whereby distinct 'bits' of information are collected together perceptually
and cognitively into larger, coordinated wholes, or 'chunks')
cicatrization, cicatrization instinct
circadian-rhythms, circadian-rhythms instincts
circumspection, circumspection instinct
civilian catastrophe reaction, civilian-catastrophe-reaction instinct
clairvoyance, clairvoyance instinct
clamor, clamor instinct
clapping, clapping-your-hands instinct

clarion, clarion-call instinct

clash, two-or-more-colors-clash instinct

clash, two-or-more-styles-clash instinct

classical, classical-conditioning instincts (Note: All instincts are learning instincts; "classical conditioning" is only a kind of instinctual learning. Example: Humans have many fear instincts; perhaps all instincts are fear instincts. The number of possible phobias is perhaps limited only by the number of normal instincts. Fear instincts cause fear; "classical fear conditioning" does not cause fear, as traditional psychology believes.

classification, a-genius-for-verbal-classification instinct

classification, classification instinct

classify, the-urge-to-classify-the-elements-of-the-environment instinct

classify, to-classify-people-into-friends-and-aliens instinct

claustrophobia, claustrophobia (fear of closed spaces) instinct

clean, the-urge-to-keep-ourselves-clean instinct

clear, to-clear-one's-throat instinct

clench, to-clench-your-fist-because-you-are-angry instinct

clench, to-clench-your-teeth-because-you-are-angry instinct

climb, the-urge-to-climb-trees instinct

cling, infants-(often)-cling,-grasp,-grab,-and-do-whatever-else-they-can-to-stay-close-to-their-parents instinct

cling, the-cling-and-feed-reaction-of-the-newborn instinct

clinging, clinging instinct (children is running to the parent and clinging)

clinging, clinging-response instinct (the baby's body movements are remains of the ancestral primate clinging response)

clique, clique instinct

clocks, biological-clocks instincts

closeness, closeness (intimacy, supportiveness, etc) instincts

closure, the-principle-of-closure instinct (the-viewer-perceives-incomplete-figures-as-complete-wholes)

clustering, clustering instinct

coaxing, coaxing-voice instinct

cocktail party phenomenon, cocktail-party-phenomenon instinct

coddle, to-coddle-our-friends instinct

coercion, coercion instinct

cogitating, cogitating instinct

cognition, cognition instincts

cognitive, cognitive-map instinct

cognitive, cognitive-reflex instincts (= *reflexive*-mental-process instincts, as opposed to *reflective*-mental-process instincts)

coin, to-pay-someone-back-in-their-own-coin instinct

cold shoulder, to-give-someone-the-cold-shoulder instinct (Psychologists have found that *the cold shoulder* (social ostracism) is much more common than anyone supposed. 75 per cent of respondents said that they had been ostracized by a loved one, while 68 per cent admitted ostracizing a close friend or relative. Men and women are equally likely to be both perpetrators and victims. Ostracism usually involves not talking and avoiding eye contact.)

cold stare, to-give-somebody-a-cold-stare instinct

cold sweat, the-cold-sweat-of-fear instinct

cold, to-feel-cold instinct

coldness, coldness instinct

coldness, coldness-in-one's-voice instinct

coldness, the-sensing-of-coldness instinct

collecting, collecting instinct

color, a-strong-preference-for-foods-with-colors-of-ripe-nuts,-fruits-and-roots instinct

color, color-experiences (colors, hue, saturation, luminance, etc) instincts

color, the-emotional-aspects-of-normal-color-vision instincts (e.g. color fascinates all of us)

colors, to-judge-blue-and-green-as-'cold'-colors instinct

colors, to-judge-red-and-yellow-as-'warm'-colors instinct

combat, combat instinct

combat, the-passions-aroused-by-combat instinct

combat fatigue, combat-fatigue instinct (gross-stress-reaction instinct)

combination tone, combination-tone instinct
come hither, 'come hither'-look instinct
comedy, comedy instinct
comfort, comfort instinct
comfort, to-comfort-someone instinct
comfortable, to-feel-comfortable instinct
comforting, comforting-movements (e.g. swaying rhythmically from side to side) instinct
comforting, comforting-vocalizations instinct
comic, comic instinct
commiseration, commiseration instinct
commitment, commitment instinct
committed, the-more-emotional-the-behavior,-the-more-committed-that-person-is-to-what-is-being-said instinct
common chemical sense, common chemical sense, the-emotional-aspects-of-the-common-
common sense, common-sense instincts
communicate, a-general-urge-to-communicate instinct
communicating, communicating-feelings-and-ideas instincts
comparing, comparing instinct
compass, magnetic-compass instinct
compassion, compassion instinct
compassion, compassion-elicits-reciprocal-compassion instinct
compensation, compensation instinct
competent, we-tend-to-be-attracted-to-competent-people instinct
competition, between-group-competition instinct
competition, competition instinct
competitive, competitive-ambition instinct
complacency, complacency instinct
complaining, complaining instinct
compliment, to-compliment-someone instinct
compunction, compunction instinct

computerphobia, computerphobia (fear of computers or using them) instincts (also called cyberphobia)

comradeship, comradeship instinct

concealment, concealment instinct

conceit, conceit instinct

concentrate, ability-to-concentrate-on-things instinct (children with ADHD cannot concentrate for more than a few seconds)

concentration, absorbed-concentration instinct

concentration, deep-concentration instinct

concept, concept-formation instincts

conception, conception instinct

concepts, basic-innate-concepts instincts (e.g. concepts like *red, purple, large, small*)

concern, concern instinct

concern, genuine-concern-for-others instinct

concerned, a-concerned-facial-expression instinct

concession, concession instinct (normal behavior needs to be explained!)

conciliation, conciliation instinct

concord, concord (harmonious relationship between tones sounding together) instincts

condemnation, condemnation instinct

condescending, to-be-condescending instinct

condescending, to-be-theatrically-condescending instinct

conditioned, conditioned-learning instinct

confabulate, confabulate instinct

confidence, confidence instinct

confined, confined spaces, dread-of-confined-spaces instinct

conflict (serious disagreement), the-emotional-aspects-of-a-conflict instinct

conflict, to-solve-conflict-by-aggression instinct

conform, humans-conform-to-their-culture instinct (conformity is decided by a desire and a desire is an instinct)

conformity, a-predisposition-to-conformity-and-consecration instinct

conformity, conformity instincts
confrontation, confrontation instinct
congratulation, congratulation instinct
conjure, to-conjure-something-up instinct
connectedness, desire-for-social-connectedness instinct
conquering, conquering instinct (instincts are situational!)
conscience, conscience instinct
conscientiousness, conscientiousness instinct
conscious, conscious-self-awareness instinct
consciousness, consciousness instincts (There is nothing we know about more directly than consciousness, but it is extraordinarily hard to reconcile it with everything else we know. However, all instincts have a conscious component)
consciousness, divided-consciousness instincts (Example: driving *and* thinking about sex)
consciousness, focused-consciousness instinct (=directed-consciousness instinct)
consciousness, loosely-drifting-consciousness instinct (= flowing-consciousness instinct)
consciousness, normal-waking-consciousness instincts
consciousness, the-immediate-experience-that-consciousness-is-a-singular instinct
consecration, consecration instinct
consent, consent instinct (normal behavior needs to be explained!)
conservation, the-concept-of-conservation instinct
conservatism, conservatism instinct
considering, considering instinct (reflection instinct)
consolation, consolation instinct
consonance, consonance (harmonious blending or fusion of tones) instinct
constancy, the-principle-of-brightness-constancy instinct
constancy, the-principle-of-color-constancy instinct
constancy, the-principle-of-shape-constancy instinct

constancy, the-principle-of-size-constancy instinct

consternation, consternation instinct

contact comfort, contact-comfort instinct

contagion, behavioral-or-emotional-contagion instinct (e.g. one child may faint when dissecting in a biology lesson, promptly followed by numbers of others)

contemplation, contemplation instinct

contempt, to-have-contempt-for-someone-or-something instincts

contention, contention instinct

contentment, contentment instinct

contest, contest instinct

continuity, the-principle-of-continuity instinct (the viewer tends to perceive continuity in lines and patterns)

contra-suggestibility, contra-suggestibility instinct (a tendency (seemingly possessed by all children) to take a position counter to or opposite to one which has been suggested)

control, desire-to-control-others instinct

control, keeping-self-control instinct

control, to-control-one's-impulses instinct

control, to-control-one's-own-feelings instinct

control, you-are-in-control:-palms-turned-downwards instinct

controlling, controlling-motor-activity instincts

convergent, convergent-thinking instinct

conversation, to-enjoy-conversation instinct

conversion, a-moment-of-religious-conversion instinct

conviction, firm-convictions-and-established-beliefs instinct

conviction, ideological-convictions instinct

cooing, cooing-voice instinct

cool, a-color-that-is-cool instinct

Coolidge effect, Coolidge-effect instinct (= following intercourse, males will have intercourse again with the same receptive female some time after the refractory period has elapsed)

cooperation, cooperation-based-on-reciprocity instinct
cooperativeness, cooperativeness instinct
coordination, eye-hand coordination
coprophobia, coprophobia (fear of feces/dirt/filth/contamination) instincts
copulation, copulation instincts (privacy is sought, kissing, licking, sucking, biting, soft nibbling, gentle nipping, lubrication, increasing pulse rate, increasing blood pressure, erection, penis insertion, sexual flush, gasping, moaning, grunting, fighting for air, climax: the face may be contorted, with mouth wide open and nostrils expanded, ejaculation, exhaustion, relaxation, rest, sleep)
coquetry, coquetry instinct
cosiness, cosiness instinct
count, we-all-want-to-count-for-something instinct
counter, counter-attack instinct
counter, counter-threat instinct
counteraction, counteraction-need instinct
counterphobic, counterphobic-character instinct
courage, courage instincts
courage, mental-courage instincts
courage, physical-courage instincts
courtesy, courtesy instinct
courtliness, courtliness instinct
courtship, courtship-and-pre-copulatory-sequence instincts (a distinctive vocalization tone, murmuring sweet nothings, hand-to-hand, arm-to-arm, mouth-to-face, mouth-to-mouth, embracing, running, chasing, jumping, dancing, juvenile play patterns, courtship feeding…)
covetousness, covetousness instinct
cowardice, cowardice instinct (may sometimes be a survival instinct!)
cowed, to-be-cowed instinct
cowering, cowering instinct
coyness, coyness instinct

cradle, mothers-cradle-their-infants-in-their-left-arm,-next-to-their-hearts instinct (left-handed mothers behave in the same way)

craft, craft instinct

crawling-walking, crawling-walking instincts

creasing, creasing-the-forehand-when-you-are-puzzled instinct

creation, artistic-creation instincts

creation, creation instincts

creative, to-be-happy-about-creative-activity instinct

creativeness, creativeness instincts

creativity, creativity instincts (It is possible to be highly creative without being highly intelligent, and vice versa)

credulity, credulity instinct (Credulity is the man's weakness, but the child's strength. Charles Lamb)

creed, creed instincts

creep, to-creep instinct (people *and* animals creep)

cringe, to-cringe instinct

critical, critical-thinking instinct

criticism, criticism instinct

criticism, indignant-criticism instinct

criticism, the-need-to-defend-oneself-from-criticism instinct

criticize, to-criticize-heartlessness instinct

criticize, to-criticize-someone-or-something instinct

criticizing, the-pleasure-of-criticizing instinct

crooked, the-one-sided-crooked-smile instinct

crouch, to-crouch-down-because-you-are-frightened-or-are-hiding-from-someone instinct

crouching, the-basic-submissive-response-of-crouching-and-screaming instinct

crow, to-crow-about-or-over-something instinct

crowd, to-crowd-someone instinct

crowded, to-feel-crowded instinct

cruelty, cruelty instinct

crushed, to-be-crushed instinct
cry, a-frantic-cry instinct
cry, to-cry instinct (when you cry, you produce tears)
cry, to-cry-out instinct
cry, to-cry-with-laughter instinct
crying, baby's-crying instinct (newborn babies cry but they do not weep)
crying, crying-fearfully instinct
cuddle, a-baby-must-be-cuddled-a-lot instinct
cuddle, we-want-to-cuddle-an-infant instinct
cues, to-interpret-social-cues instincts
culture, the-capacity-for-culture instincts
cunnilingus, cunnilingus instinct
cup, to-cup-one's-ear-to-hear-better instinct
cupidity, cupidity instinct
curb, to-curb-someone instinct
curiosity, curiosity instinct
curiosity, to-show-curiosity-toward-strangers instinct
curse, to-curse-someone instinct
curse, to-curse-something instinct
cursed, to-be-cursed instinct
cursory, a-cursory-glance instinct
curved, the-sight-of-a-slender-curved-shape-lying-flat-on-the-path-ahead-of-us-is-sufficient-to-elicit-defensive-fear-responses instinct
cussedness, cussedness instinct
custom, attachment-to-custom-and-tradition instinct
customary, customary-behavior instinct
cut off, cut-off instincts (e.g. 'nervous breakdown', eye-screening at moments of deep concentration, he/she shuts his/her eyes tightly as he/she searches his/her memory, looks away for unusually long periods, keeps glancing away and then back again rapidly, struggling to open and shut his/her eyes at the same time (the stuttering eye))

cutaneous senses, the-emotional-aspects-of-cutaneous-senses-for-contact,-pressure,-cold,-warmth,-and-pain instincts

cutting, a-cutting-remark instinct

cyberphobia, cyberphobia (fear of computers or using them) instincts (also called computerphobia)

cynically, to-smile-cynically instinct

cynicism, cynicism instinct

cynophobia, cynophobia (fear of dogs) instinct

cypridophobia, cypridophobia (fear of venereal disease/sexual activity in general) instincts

D

d, the-*d*-speech-sounds instinct (The *d* speech sounds are the minimal units of instinctual speech sounds that correspond roughly to the letter *d* of the alphabet)

damaged, damaged instincts (due to gene damage) SCIENCE DON'T RECOGNIZE THE GENETIC CATASTROPHE, WHY ???

damn, just-not-giving-a-damn-any-more instinct

dancing, dancing instinct

dancing, dancing-eyes instinct

dancing, dancing-mania instinct

dandyism, dandyism instinct

danger, avoiding-danger instinct

danger, refusing-to-recognize-a-real-danger instinct

danger, to-feel-danger instinct

daredevil, daredevil instinct

dark, dark-and-light-adaptation-of-the-eye instinct (note: seeing *is* behavior; reflexes are instincts, but instincts are not reflexes)

darkness, fear-of-darkness-or-of-night instinct

dastardly, a-dastardly-action instinct

dawdling, dawdling intinct

day-dreaming, day-dreaming instinct

dazzle, someone-or-something-dazzles-you instinct

death, death-feigning instinct (immobility instinct)

deceit, a-smile-of-deceit instinct

decency, decency instinct

decent, decent-feelings instinct

decentered, decentered-thinking instinct (thinking of more than one thing at a time)

deception, calculated-deception instinct

deception, deception instinct

decision, decision-making-and-emotion-go-together instinct

decisions, to-make-calculated-decisions-about-something instinct

decisiveness, decisiveness instinct

declaim, to-declaim instinct

decoration, decoration instinct

decoration, we-are-quite-prone-to-leaping-to-conclusions-about-some-one's-status,-social-strata,-trustworthiness,-and-overall-character-from-body-decorations instinct

decorum, to-behave-with-decorum instinct

dedication, dedication instinct

deduction, deduction instinct

defamation, defamation instinct (=defaming instinct)

defeat, the-postures-of-defeat (the head is lowered etc.) instinct

defecation, private-defecation instinct

defend, the-need-to-defend-oneself instinct

defend, to-defend-someone-or-something instinct

defending, defending-his/her-own-individual-home-base instinct

defense, defense-mechanisms instincts (projection, denial, reaction for-mation, regression, rationalization, displacement, sublimation, repression, intellectualization)

defense, defense-reaction instinct

defense, group-defense-of-territory instinct

deference, deference-behavior instinct (to admire and defer to a leader or superior)

defiance, defiance instinct

deindividuation, deindividuation (what often occurs in mobs when individual choice is submerged in mob action) instinct

dejection, dejection instinct

delectation, delectation instinct

deliberation, deliberation instinct

delight, delight instinct

delighted, delighted-when-friends-and-acquaintances-enjoy-good-fortune instinct

delinquency, delinquency instinct

delinquency, juvenile-delinquency instinct

delusion, delusion instinct

demand, to-demand instinct

demean, to-demean-someone-or-something instinct

demophobia, demophobia (dread-of-crowds) instinct

denigrate, our-villingness-to-denigrate-*any*-group-that-exists-outside-our-own instinct

denigration, denigration instinct

denunciation, denunciation instinct

depreciation, the-need-to-counteract-depreciation-of-self instinct

depressed, to-be-depressed instinct (= feeling-depressed instinct)

deprivation, a-sense-of-deprivation instinct

depth, depth-perception instinct (is accomplished by using a number of two-dimensional visual cues to create a perceptual distance)

depths, dread-of-depths instinct

derision, derision instinct

derogatory, a-derogatory-remark-or-comment instinct

deserves, "the agent deserves praise or blame" instinct

designs, preferred-visual-designs instinct

desire, you-desire-something instincts (see each individual desire)
desolation, desolation (a feeling of great unhappiness and despair) instinct
despair, despair instinct
desperation, desperation instinct
despondency, despondency instinct
detection, detection instincts
detection, detection-of-cheating instinct
detection, pattern-detection instincts
determination, determination instinct (to-be-determined instinct)
determination, self-determination instincts
deterrence, deterrence instinct
detest, you-detest-someone-or-something instincts
detraction, detraction instinct
devotion, devotion instinct
devotion, devotion-to-duty instinct
dexterity, dexterity instincts
dexterity, manual-dexterity instincts
diction, diction instinct
diet, the-urge-to-seek-a-varied-diet instinct
dietary, dietary-preference instinct
diffidence, diffidence instinct
dignify, to-dignify-someone-or-something instinct
dignity, the-sense-of-dignity instinct
digression, digression instinct (= to-digress instinct)
dilation, pupil-dilation/constriction-signals instincts
diligence, diligence instinct
direction, a-sense-of-direction instinct
dirt, dread-of-dirt instinct
dirty, dirty-jokes instinct
dirty, to-say-and-do-dirty-things instinct
disagreement, disagreement-cause-anger instinct
disappointment, disappointment instinct

disapproval, disapproval instincts

disapproval, moral-disapproval instinct

disaster, disaster-victims-revert-to-behavior-stemming-from-their-infancy instinct

discharge, discharge-of-affect (the diminishing of experienced affect by displaying and expressing it) instinct

discipline, discipline instincts

discomfiture, discomfiture instinct

discomfort, discomfort instinct

discomfort, to-adjust-to-discomfort instinct

discontent, discontent instinct

discourage, discourage instinct

discouraged, to-become-discouraged instinct

discourtesy, discourtesy instinct

discreet, discreet-behavior instinct

discrimination, discrimination instincts

discrimination, pattern-discrimination instincts

discussion, discussion instinct

disdain, to-feel-disdain-for-someone-or-something instinct

disease, dread-of-some-particular-disease instinct

diseases, the-brain-and-immune-system-continuously-signal-each-other-and-influence-how-well-we-resist-or-recover-from-infectious-or-innflammatory-diseases instincts

disgrace, disgrace instinct

disgust, disgust-that-makes-you-spit-out-bad-tasting-food instinct

disgust, to-feel-disgust instinct

dishonesty, dishonesty instinct

dishonor, dishonor instinct

disillusionment, disillusionment instinct

disinclination, disinclination instinct

disingenuity, disingenuity instinct

disinhibition, disinhibition (seeking sensation through social activities such as parties) instinct

disinterest, disinterest instinct

dislike, dislike instinct

disloyality, disloyality instinct

dismay, dismay instinct

disobedience, genuine-disobedience instinct (exists?)

disparagement, disparagement instinct

displacements-activities, displacements-activities instincts (Displacement activities appear in almost any situation of stress and tension. Examples: (displacement) feeding, rubbing our chins, rubbing our hands together, licking our lips, scratching our heads, 'washing' our faces with our hands, biting our nails, stroking our ear-lobes, cleaning our ear-passages, rubbing our noses, picking our noses, blowing our noses, sniffing our noses, tugging at our beards or moustaches, fumbling, fiddling, fidgeting, sipping, nibbling, displacement-yawning, tidying, adjusting. Many animals also show displacement activities when in states of conflict) displacement-sleeping, displacement-sleeping instinct (soldiers experienced an almost overwhelming desire to sleep at the moment they were ordered in to the attack; this is an instinct we share with certain species of birds)

display, sexual-display instinct

dispute, dispute instinct (instincts are situational!)

dispute, indignant-dispute instinct

dispute, voices-raised-in-dispute instinct

disputes, family-disputes instinct (instincts are situational!)

disquiet, disquiet instinct

dissatisfaction, dissatisfaction instinct

dissonance, dissonance (unpleasant effect of two tones sounded simultaneously, which do not blend or fuse) instinct

dissonance, the-reduction-of-cognitive-dissonance instinct

distance, keeping-your-distance (defending your personal space) instinct

distances, to-judge-distances instinct

distortion, systematic-distortion-of-memory-for-past-events-by-defensive-or-repressive-operations instincts

distracted, to-be-distracted instinct

distractibility, distractibility (capable of being distracted) instinct

distraught, distraught instinct

distress, distress instinct

distrust, distrust instinct

divergent, divergent-thinking instinct

diversity, to-enjoy-diversity instinct

divide, to-divide-the-world's-people-into-"us"-and-"them" instinct

divorce, divorce instinct (Helen Fisher has argued that divorce is an adaptation)

docility, docility instinct

dodge, to-dodge instinct

doggedness, doggedness instinct

doggo, to-lie-doggo instinct

dogmatism, dogmatism instinct

dominance, dominance-hierarchy instincts

dominant, males-are-dominant-over-females-in-human-hunter-gatherer-societies instincts

dominant, the-dominant-eye instinct

dominate, you-dominate-a-person-or-a-group-of-people instinct

doodle, to-doodle instinct

dormancy, dormancy instinct

doting, doting instinct

double standard, the-double-standard-of-in-group-morality-and-out-group-ferocity instinct

doubt, doubt instinct

dozing, dozing instinct

drawl, to-drawl instinct

dread, dread instinct

dream, dream instincts (the dream instincts are the ordinary instincts working during sleep!)

    dream, to-held-on-to-the-dream-of-something instinct

    dreamy, a-dreamy-expression-on-someone's-face instinct

    drool, to-drool-over-someone-or-something instinct

    drowse, to-drowse instinct

    drowsiness, drowsiness instinct

    dry mouth, the-dry-mouth-of-incipient-attack instinct

    dubitation, dubitation instinct

    dubitations, painful-dubitations instinct

    dumbfounded, to-be-dumbfounded instinct

    dumbstruck, to-be-dumbstruck instinct

    duty, a-sense-of-duty instinct

    duty, a-sense-of-duty-to-the-group instinct

dysmorphophobia, dysmorphophobia (fear of imagined defects in appearance) instinct

E

e, the-*e*-speech-sounds instinct (The *e* speech sounds are the minimal units of instinctual speech sounds that correspond roughly to the letter *e* of the alphabet)

ear lobe, ear-lobe-stimulation instinct (there are cases on record of both males and females actually reaching orgasm as a result of ear-lobe stimulation)

    earnestness, earnestness instinct

    ears, to-be-all-ears instinct

    ease, to-feel-at-ease instinct

    eating, eating instinct

    ebullience, ebullience instinct

echo, to-respond-with-feelings-of-warmth-towards-those-who-echo-our-postures-and-our-body-movements instinct ecstasy, ecstasy instinct

ecstatic, an-ecstatic-facial-expression instinct

edgy, a-person-gets-edgy instinct

edification, edification instinct

educate, to-educate-someone instinct

effervescence, effervescence instinct

effort, an-investment-of-effort instinct

effrontery, effrontery instinct

egalitarianism, egalitarianism instinct

egocentricity, egocentricity instinct

egoism, egoism instinct (egotism instinct)

egomania, egomania instinct

eh, 'eh' instinct (you say 'eh' when you are asking someone to reply to you or to agree with you)

eidetic, eidetic-imagery instinct

ejaculation, ejaculation-urge instinct

elaboration, elaboration (the process of creating associations between a new memory and existing memories) instinct

elaboration, the-elaboration-of-an-idea instinct

elation, elation (intense joyful excitement) instinct

elegance, the-emotional-aspects-of-elegance instinct

emancipatory, emancipatory striving instinct

embarrassment, embarrassment instinct

embellishment, embellishment instinct

embrace,   an-urge-to-smile-at,-touch,-caress,-embrace-and-care-for-the-baby instinct

embracing, embracing behavior instinct

embroider, you-embroider-something instinct

emotional, emotional-sweating (on the palms of the hands, the soles of the feet, the armpits and the forehead) instinct emotionally charged, so-attuned-are-humans-to-emotionally-charged-events-that-we-eagerly-seek-them-out,-even-if-they-don't-directly-relate-to-us instinct

emotions in others, the-perception-of-emotions-in-others instinct

empathy, empathy instinct

emptiness, a-feeling-of-emptiness instinct

emulation, emulation instinct

enamoured, you-are-enamoured-of-a-person instinct

enamoured, you-are-enamoured-of-something instinct

enchantment, enchantment instinct

encouragement, encouragement instinct

encouragement, giving-cries-of-encouragement instinct

endearment, endearment instinct

endurance, endurance instincts

enervated, to-feel-enervated instinct

enissophobia, enissophobia (fear of criticism) instinct

enjoyment, a-sense-of-self-enjoyment instinct

enjoyment, enjoyment instinct

enjoyment, enjoyment-of-being-with-other-people instinct

enjoyment, enjoyment-of-excitement instinct (this is perhaps only an aspect of the excitement instinct)

enlarged, enlarged-pupils-are-appealing instinct

enmity, enmity instinct

ennui, ennui instinct

ennui, the-mood-of-ennui instinct

ensnare, you-ensnare-someone instinct

entertain, the-need-to-entertain-others instinct

entertainment, self-entertainment instinct

entertainment, to-enjoy-entertainment instinct

enthusiasm, enthusiasm instinct

enticement, enticement instinct

entrepreneurship, entrepreneurship instinct

envy, envy instinct

epistemophobia, epistemophobia (fear of knowledge) instinct

equilibrium sense, the-behavioral-aspects-of-the-equilibrium-sense instinct

erect, erect-posture instinct (postures are behavior)

erection, to-be-aroused-to-erection instinct

eremophobia, eremophobia (fear of solitude/being alone) instincts

ereuthrophobia, ereuthrophobia (fear of blushing) instinct

ergasiophobia, ergasiophobia (fear of work/responsibility) instincts (also called ergophobia)

ergophobia, ergophobia (fear of work/responsibility) instincts (also called ergasiophobia)

erotic arousal, erotic-arousal-pattern instincts

erotic love, erotic-love-play instincts

eroticism, eroticism (sexual excitement arising from areas other than the genitals) instincts

erotophobia, erotophobia (fear of sex) instinct

erythrophobia, erythrophobia (fear of red objects/blushing) instincts

esprit, esprit-de-corps instinct

esteem, esteem instinct

ethical, ethical instincts

ethical, ethical-code instinct

ethical, ethical-conflict instinct

ethnocentrism, ethnocentrism instinct

etiquette, etiquette instinct

euphoria, euphoria instinct (=a-sense-of-euphoria instinct)

euphoria, the-euphoria-of-sudden-love instinct

euphoric, a-euphoric-high instinct

even, to-get-even-with-someone instinct

evil, a-sense-of-the-idea-of-evil instinct

evil, evil-thoughts instinct

evil, to-be-evil instinct (someone who is evil takes pleasure in doing things that harm other people)

exaggerated, exaggerated-strutting-walk instinct
exalt, to-exalt-someone instinct
exaltation, exaltation instinct
exaltation, exaltation-from-discovery instinct
exaltation, religious-exaltation instinct
exasperation, exasperation instinct
excitability, general-excitability instinct
excitable, excitable-runs instinct
excite, the-need-to-excite-others instinct
excitement, excitement-seeking instinct
excitement, nervous-excitement instinct
excitement, the-sheer-excitement-of-vivid-experience instinct
exclamation, exclamation instinct
exclusion, the-automatic-exclusion-of-sexual-bonding-between-individu-als-who-have-previously-formed-certain-other-kinds-of-relationship instinct
excuse, to-excuse-your-behavior instinct
exhaustion, a-feeling-of-exhaustion instinct
exhibitionism, exhibitionism instinct
exhilaration, exhilaration instinct
exhorting, exhorting instinct
existential, existential-anxiety instinct
expectancy, expectancy instinct
expectancy, tense-expectancy instinct
expectation, expectation instinct
expectations, to-live-up-to-the-expectations-of-those-around-us instinct
experience, seeking-novel-experiences-through-the-mind-and-senses instinct
expiation, expiation instinct
explanation, explanation instinct
expletive, expletive instinct (an expletive is a rude word or expression which you say loudly and suddenly when you are annoyed, excited, or in pain)
exploratory, exploratory-behavior instinct

exploratory, exploratory-talking instinct

explosions, emotional-explosions instinct

explosive, an-explosive-temper instinct

exposition, exposition-need (need to explain, demonstrate and lecture others) instinct

expostulation, expostulation instinct

expressiveness, expressiveness instinct

extinction, extinction (the process of unlearning) instincts (remember: all instincts are learning instincts)

extravagance, extravagance instinct

extraversion, extraversion/introversion instinct

extremism, extremism instinct

exuberance, exuberance instinct

exultation, exultation instinct

exultation, exultation-of-victory instinct

eye, eye-hand-coordination instinct

eye, eye-movements instincts

eye, something-catches-your-eye instinct

eyebrow flash, the-eyebrow-flash-used-as-part-of-a-friendly-greeting-or-a-flirtation instinct (The eyebrow flash is a rapid raising of the eyebrows lasting about 1/6 of a second. It is a universal sign of either greeting or flirtation.)

eyebrows, elevation-of-the-eyebrows instinct

eyebrows, people-raise-their-eyebrows-at the-center-of-their-forehead-to-duplicate-the-forlorn-look-of-grief-and-distress instinct

eyebrows, raising-eyebrows-in-surprise instinct

eyes, narrowing-the-eyes instinct

eyes, the-automatic-movement-of-the-eyes-to-keep-them-fixed-on-an-object-as-the-head-moves instinct

eyes, the-automatic-movement-of-the-head-to-better-orient-the-ears-to-a-sound instinct eyes, the-eyes-cast-downwards-when-you-are-upset-or-shy-or-hiding-something instincts

eyes, to-be-all-eyes instinct

eyes, to-lower-one's-eyes instinct

eyes, to-make-eyes-at-someone instinct (you look at them in a way that indicates that you are attracted to them)

F

f, the-*f*-speech-sounds instinct (The *f* speech sounds are the minimal units of instinctual speech sounds that correspond roughly to the letter *f* of the alphabet)

face, face-recognition instinct

faces, to-make-faces-at-somebody instinct

faces, to-remember-faces instinct

facial, facial-expressions instincts (e.g. a happy face, an unhappy face, a sad face, a serious face, a brave face, a smiling face, a laughing face, a straight face, a shut face, a pulled face, a good face, a puzzled face ... a human has about seven thousand facial expressions)

facial, 'facial vision' (echolocation) instinct

facial, the-importance-of-facial-beauty instinct

facial, to-interpret-facial-expressions instinct

faction, faction (e.g. political faction) instinct

faddishness, faddishness instinct

faeces, dread-of-faeces instincts

faint hearted, faint-hearted-behavior instinct

fairness, fairness instinct (= a-sense-of-fairness instinct)

fairness, judging-the-fairness-of-social-bargains-and-the-sincerity-of-social-offers instinct

faith, faith (a strong religious belief) instinct

faith, faith-in-someone-or-something instinct

faithful, being-faithful-to-our-spouses instinct
faithfulness, faithfulness instinct
faithlessness, faithlessness instinct
fake, a-fake-smile instinct
fake, people-can-distinguish-a-fake-smile-from-a-real-one instinct
fake, to-fake-a-feeling,-emotion,-or-reaction instinct
fall, someone-falls-to-their-knees instinct
fall, to-fall-in-love instinct
fall, to-fall-on-each-other-in-delight-and-tears instinct
fall, to-fall-out-of-love instinct
fall back, to-fall-back instinct (you move quickly away from someone because they have upset or frightened you)
falling asleep, falling-asleep instinct
falls on, someone-falls-on-you instinct (they hug you and embrace you because they are very happy or excited)
fame, a-passion-for-fame instinct
familiarity, familiarity-feeling instinct
families, the-predisposition-to-assemble-into-families instinct
family, family-territory instinct
family, family's-warmth (e.g. cohesion, expressiveness) instinct
famished, to-feel-famished instinct
fan, fan instinct
fan, to-fan-a-feeling instinct
fanaticism, fanaticism instinct
fanaticism, "youthful fanaticism" instinct
fancy, fancy (uncontrolled imagination) instinct
fantasies, sexual-fantasies instinct
fantasize, to-fantasize instinct
fantasize, to-fantasize-when-making-love instinct
fascination, fascination instinct
fashion, fashion instinct
fastidiousness, fastidiousness instinct

fatigue, a-feeling-of-fatigue instinct (feeling is behavior; fatigue is an inborn warning mechanism)

favor, to-do-somebody-a-favor instinct

favoritism, favoritism instinct

fear, ability-to-control-fear instinct

fear, fear instinct

fear, fear-of-failure instinct

fear, the-fear-face instinct

fear, the-infants-fear-of-being-separated-from-their-caregivers instinct

fear, the-infants'-fear-of-strangers instinct

fear, the-scream-of-fear instinct

fearfulness, fearfulness instinct

fearless, apparently-fearless-rage instinct

fearlessness, fearlessness instinct

feasting, feasting instinct

febrile, febrile-behavior instinct

febriphobia, febriphobia (fear of fever/body dysfunction produced by a rise in body temperature) instincts

fed up, to-be-fed-up instinct

feed, people-gather-together-to-feed instinct

feeding, feeding-behavior instinct (eating instinct)

feeding, feeding-pace instinct

feel bad, to-feel-bad-about-something-that-has-happened instinct

feel bad, to-feel-bad-about-something-that-you-have-done instinct

feeling, feeling-impatient:-tapping-a-foot-on-the-ground instinct

feigning, death-feigning instinct (= immobility instinct)

felicity, felicity instinct

fellatio, fellatio instinct

fellow, fellow-feeling instinct

fellowship, a-feeling-of-fellowship instinct (= fellowship-feeling instinct)

fellowship, fellowship instinct

female beauty, men-desire-women-with-full-lips-and-small-chins instinct feminine, feminine-coyness instinct

femininity, femininity instincts (all of the women's learning instincts are feminine, more or less)

ferment, ferment instinct

ferocity, ferocity instinct

fertile, to-be-attracted-to-fertile-females instinct

fervent, to-be-fervent-about-something instinct

fervor, fervor-for-something instinct

festivity, festivity instinct

fetishism, fetishism instinct

feud, blood-feuds instinct

feuding, factional-feuding instinct

feuding, feuding instinct

feverish, feverish-emotion instinct

fib, fib instinct

fickleness, fickleness instinct

fiction, the-exquisite-enjoyment-of-fiction instinct

fictionalization, fictionalization instinct

fiddle, to-fiddle-with-something (because you are nervous or bored) instinct

fidelity, fidelity instinct

fidget, to-fidget instinct

fight, intellectual-fight instinct

fight, stand-up-fight instinct

fight, to-fight-an-emotion-or-desire instinct (e.g. to fight the urge to cry)

fight, to-fight-back instinct

fighting, fighting instincts (e.g. using the hands to grasp and squeeze, using the legs to kick, using the body to ram, bump and push, arm-blows and wrestling holds, scratching, tearing of hair, biting, ungainly grappling on the ground, scuffling, killing)

fighting, male-fighting instinct

fighting, play-fighting instinct

fighting, you-are-fighting-with-yourself instinct (this is a special kind of instinct competition)

figure-background, the-viewer's-figure-background-organization instinct

figure out, the-impulsive-desire-to-figure-everything-out instinct

filial, filial-devotion instinct

find fault, to-find-fault-with-something-or-someone instinct

finger, to-point-a-finger-at-someone instinct

fingers, separate-control-in-the-fingers instinct

firm, to-be-firm instinct

firmness, firmness instinct

first, your-first-reaction-to-something instinct

first sight, the-love-at-first-sight instinct

fist, shaking-a-fist-at-someone instinct

fistfights, the-fistfights instinct

fists, to-shout-and-shake-our-fists-at-one-another-when-we-are-angry instinct

fixation, fixation (a strong attachment to an idea, theory, another person, etc.) instinct

fixation, the-eyes-maintain-fixation instinct

fixed, fixed-idea instinct (insistent-idea instinct)

flaming, flaming (a mild swear word) instinct

flash, to-flash-a-look-or-a-smile-at-someone instinct

flash, your-thoughts-flash-back-to-something instinct

flashbulb, flashbulb-memories instinct

flashpoint, emotional-flashpoint instinct

flat, to-say-something-in-a-flat-voice instinct

flattery, flattery instinct

flattery, to-be-warmed-by-flattery instinct

flaunting, flaunting-instinct

flaunting, flaunting-his/her-superiority instinct

flavor, sensing-a-flavor instinct (sensing is behavior)

flavor, the-emotional-aspects-of-flavor instinct

flee, ready-to-flee instinct

fleeing, fleeing instinct

flehman, flehman (a lip curl associated with sniffing) instinct

flicker, a-flicker-of-emotion-or-feeling instinct

flicking, the-rapid-flicking-action-of-the-hand-when-ridding-yourself-of-small-creatures-making-contact-with-your-skin instinct

flight, flight-from-reality instinct

flinching, flinching instinct

fling, to-fling-a-remark-at-someone instinct

flirtation, flirtation instinct

flirtatiousness, flirtatiousness instinct

flounce, to-flounce-somewhere instinct (you, usually a woman, walk quickly, with exaggerated movements, in a way which suggests that you are angry or upset)

fluctuations, fluctuations-of-attention instinct

flush, flush instinct

flutter, your-heart-or-stomach-flutters instinct

foaming, foaming-at-the-mouth (because you are very angry) instinct

focal, focal-attention instinct

focus, mental-focus instinct

focus, to-focus-your-attention instinct

foist, you-foist-something-on-someone instinct

follow, to-follow-something-with-your-eyes instinct

follower, to-be-a-follower instinct

fondle, to-fondle-someone-or-something instinct

fondness, fondness instinct

food, finding-food instinct

food, food-gathering instinct

food, food-preferences instinct

food, food-stare instinct (When food is brought to the table, it is met with *a food-stare*, especially at the moment when it is being placed on the diner's plate)

food, getting-food instinct

food, our-perception-of-food-(also-)includes-sensations-from-the-surfaces-of-the-tongue-and-mouth:-touch-and-temperature instinct

food, the-regulation-of-food-intake instinct

food, the-sight-and-aroma-of-food-greatly-affect-our-perception-of-food instinct

food, the-sight-of-food-triggers-a-desire-to-eat instinct

food, the-smell-of-food-triggers-the-desire-to-eat instinct

food, to-get-a-craving-for-a-particular-kind-of-food instinct

food, to-offer-to-share-food instinct

footpath, footpath-routes instinct (When walking on grass you always follow a ready-made track, even if it is not quite direct. Sheep do the same.)

forbearance, forbearance instinct

forbidden, forbidden-fruit-is-sweet instinct

force, the-worship-of-force instinct

forced, a-forced-smile instinct

foreboding, foreboding instinct

foreplay, the-sexual-foreplay instinct

fore-pleasure, fore-pleasure-and-end-pleasure (associated with erotic activity) instinct

foresight, foresight instinct

forethought, forethought instinct

forgetting, forgetting instinct

forgetting, motivated-forgetting instinct

forgiveness, forgiveness instinct

forgiving, to-be-forgiving instinct

forlorn, forlorn-behavior instinct

forlorn, the-forlorn-look-of-grief-and-distress

form, ability-to-recognize-by-touch-the-form-of-solid-objects instinct

forming, forming-a-habit instinct

fortitude, fortitude instinct

forward, to-look-forward-to-something instinct

foul, foul-language instinct
fracas, fracas instinct
fractiousness, fractiousness instinct
fragrance, fragrance instinct
frankness, frankness instinct
frantic, a-frantic-cry instinct
frantic, to-be-frantic instinct
fraternal, fraternal-altruism instinct
fraternity, fraternity instinct
fraternization, fraternization instinct
frazzle, to-be-worn-to-a-frazzle instinct
frazzled, you-are-frazzled instinct
free, free-association instinct
free, the-feeling-of-free-will instinct
free, to-feel-free instinct
free, to-feel-free-in-making-choices instinct
freedom, the-sense-of-freedom instinct
freemasonry, freemasonry instinct
frenetic, frenetic-activity instinct
frenzy, frenzy (violent and disorganized emotional excitement) instinct
friendliness, friendliness insstinct
friendly, the-friendly-face instinct
friends, to-partition-other-people-into-friends-and-aliens instinct
friendship, children's-friendship-groups (cliques) instinct
friendship, friendship instinct
fright, fright instinct
frightened, frightened-reaction-against-radical-innovation instinct
frivolity, frivolity instinct
frivolous, someone-is-frivolous instinct
frolic, to-frolic instinct
frostiness, frostiness instinct
frowning, frowning instinct

frozen, to-be-frozen-with-fear instinct (e.g. he heard someone coming and lay frozen)

frugality, frugality instinct

frustrated, people-who-are-frustrated-react-with-anger-and-aggression instinct

frustration, frustration instinct

full throated, full-throated-laugh instinct

full throated, full-throated-shout instinct

fun, fun instinct

fun, fun-laughing instinct

fun, fun-screaming instinct

fun, fun-smiling instinct

funny, to-have-a-funny-feeling instinct

furore, furore (a very angry or excited reaction) instinct

furtive, a-furtive-look-upon-someone's-face instinct

furtive, to-be-furtive instinct

fury, fury instinct

fuss, fuss instinct

futility, the-sense-of-futility instinct (= the-what-can-I-accomplish-any-way-feeling instinct)

G

g, the-*g*-speech-sounds instinct (The *g* speech sounds are the minimal units of instinctual speech sounds that correspond roughly to the letter *g* of the alphabet)

gaiety, gaiety instinct

gallant, to-be-gallant instinct

gallantry, gallantry instinct

gallope, to-gallope-downhill instinct

gamophobia, gamophobia (fear of marriage) instinct

gape, to-gape (to look at someone or something in surprise) instinct

gasp, to-gasp (to take a short quick breath of air in through one's mouth) instinct

gathering/hunting, women-gather,-men-hunt instincts (these genetic traits are limited to man among living primates)

gatophobia, gatophobia (fear of cats) instinct

gaze, a-concentrated-gaze instinct

gazing, gazing instinct

gender, gender-behaviors instinct

gender, gender-identity instinct

generalization, generalization instinct

generosity, generosity instinct

generosity, respect-for-generosity instinct

generosity, to-expect-reciprocal-generosity instinct

generosity, to-return-generosity instinct (reciprocal-generosity instinct)

genital, genital-eroticism instinct

genital, genital-sexual-pleasure instinct

gentle, to-be-gentle instinct

gentleman, be-gentleman/gentlewoman instinct

gentleness, gentleness instinct

geometrical, geometrical-illusions instincts

geometry, innately-given-knowledge-of-the-axioms-of-geometry instincts

gestalt, the-perception-of-gestalt instinct

gesticulations, gesticulations instinct

gesture, gesture-language instincts

get along, get-along-with-other-people instincts

get upset, get-upset instinct

geumaphobia, geumaphobia (fear of tastes) instinct

giddiness, giddiness instinct

gift, gift-giving instinct

gift, to-reciprocate-a-gift instinct

giggling, giggling instinct

gladness, gladness instinct
glamour, glamour instinct
glance, a-scrutinizing-glance instinct
glance, glance instinct
glare, glare (an angry, hard and unfriendly look or expression on someone's face) instinct
glare, to-glare-at-somebody instinct
glee, glee instinct
glee, to-laugh-with-glee instinct
gleeful, gleeful-bashing instinct
glimmering, a-glimmering-of-an-idea-or-emotion instinct
gloomy, you-are-gloomy instinct
glorification, glorification instinct
glory, glory instinct
glum, feeling-glum instinct
gluttony, gluttony instinct
gnash, to-gnash-your-teeth-in-despair instinct
go, let-yourself-go instinct
goals, to-react-according-to-a-set-of-goals-and-values instinct
goals, working-(hard-)toward-one's-goals instinct (= to-realize-your-
goals instinct)
God, the-idea-of-God instinct (= the-God(s) instinct)
goo-goo, to-goo-goo instinct (The baby of the host family crawls out to
explore, and immediately gets lifted high, to be goo-gooed at, and have its
little hands admired, and generally be messed about.)
good, a-sense-of-the-idea-of-good instinct
good, persuasive-calls-to-be-good instinct
gossip, gossip instinct
grace, grace instinct
grainy, to-sense-a-grainy-texture instinct
grammar, the-universal-grammar instinct

grasp, a-neonate-will-reflexively-grasp-anything-that-is-placed-in-its-hand instinct

grasp, to-grasp-objects instinct

grasping, grasping-reflex instinct

gratification, emotional-gratification instincts

gratification, gratification instinct

gratification, sexual-gratification instinct

gratitude, a-feeling-of-gratitude instinct

gravitation, an-innate-bias-in-favor-of-perceiving-things-to-fall-with-gravitational-acceleration instinct

greed, greed instinct

greed, to-find-greed-to-be-repugnant instinct

greediness, greediness instinct

greeting, greeting instinct

greeting, the-greeting-smile instinct

gregariousness, gregariousness instinct (herd instinct)

grief, grief instinct

grieve, to-grieve-our-dead instinct

grimace, grimace instincts

grimace, the-agonized-grimace instinct

grimace, the-grimace-of-fear instinct

grin, a-big-toothy-grin instinct

grin, a-broad-grin instinct

grin, grin instincts

grin, grin-and-bear-it instinct (women have this unique way of blocking out pain)

grinning, grinning-widely instinct

grip, the-power-grip instinct

grip, the-precision-grip instinct

groaning, groaning instinct

groom, groom-each-other instinct (grooming instinct)

groomed, the-need-to-be-groomed instinct (the hairdressing saloon is the perfect answer)

groomed, to-enjoy-looking-smart-and-well-groomed instinct

grooming, grooming-talk instinct (its function is to reinforce the greeting smile and to maintain the social togetherness)

grotesque, something-is-grotesque instinct

grouchiness, grouchiness instinct

group, a-sense-of-duty-to-the-group instinct

group, group-behavior instincts

group, group-cohesiveness instinct

group, group-contagion instinct

group, group-loyalty instinct

group, group-polarization instinct

group, group-size instincts

group, group-spirit instinct (loyalty-to-the-group instinct)

group, openness-of-group-to-others instinct

group, the-upwelling-of-anxiety-from-being-left-out-of-a-group instinct

groupishness, groupishness instinct

groups, our-ability-to-live-together-in-large-groups instinct

groups, our-tendency-to-band-together-in-groups instinct

groupthink, groupthink instinct

groveling, groveling instinct (= you-grovel instinct)

growling, growling instinct

grudge, a-sense-of-grudge instinct

grudging, a-grudging-feeling-or-behavior instinct

gruesome, something-is-gruesome instinct

gruffness, gruffness instinct

grumpy, to-be-grumpy-with-people instinct

grunting, grunting instinct

guesswork, guesswork instinct

guffaw, guffaw instinct

guiding, guiding-idea instinct (guiding-fiction instinct)

guiding, guiding-one's-children-or-grandchildren instinct
guilt, a-twinge-of-guilt instinct
guilt, the-feeling-of-guilt instinct
guilty, infants-act-guilty-after-misbehavior-and-seem-to-feel-ashamed-after-failure instinct
guilty, to-feel-guilty instinct
gulping, gulping instinct
gummy, a-gummy-smile instinct
gurgle, the-baby-gurgle-when-contended instinct
gustation, gustation instinct (= the-sense-of-taste instinct)
guts, guts instinct

H

h, the-*h*-speech-sounds instinct (The *h* speech sounds are the minimal units of instinctual speech sounds that correspond roughly to the letter *h* of the alphabet)
ha, 'ha' instinct (ha is a written form representing a sound that people make when they suddenly feel surprised or annoyed)
"ha ha ha" sounds, "ha ha ha"-laughing-sounds instinct
habit, habit instinct (to-get-into-a-particular-habit instinct)
habitat, habitat-preference instinct
habituation, nearly-any-constant-stimulus-will-produce-habituation instinct
hair, hair-erection instinct
hair, the-bristling-of-the-hair-by-terror instinct
hallowed, something-is-hallowed instinct
handedness, handedness instincts
hands, our-hands-move-as-we-speak instinct
haphephobia, haphephobia (fear of being touched by another person) instinct

happiness, facial-expressions-of-happiness instinct
happiness, happiness instinct (= a-sense-of-happiness instinct)
happiness, striving-for-personal-happiness instinct
happiness, to-value-the-happiness-of-others instinct
happy, to-be-happy-with-life instinct
harass, to-harass-the-enemy instinct
harassment, harassment instinct
hardness, hardness instinct
harm, harm-avoidance instinct (danger-avoidance instinct)
hassle, you-hassle-someone instinct (= hassling instinct)
hasty, you-are-hasty instinct
hate, to-hate instinct
hatred, hatred instinct
haughtiness, haughtiness instinct
he-man, he-man instinct
healthy, admiration-for-the-healthy,-vigorous-body instinct
hearing, the-instinctual-aspects-of-normal-hearing instincts (= hearing
instincts)
heart, to-take-something-to-heart instinct
heartbeat, the-heartbeat-sound-is-a-soothing-signal instinct
heartbreak, heartbreak instinct
hearted, to-be-warm-hearted instinct
heartless, to-be-heartless instinct
heartlessness, heartlessness instinct
heat, the-behavioral-aspects-of-heat-sensation instincts
heat, the-feeling-of-burning-heat instinct
heat, the-sensation-of-heat instinct (the-feeling-of-heat instinct)
heaving, heaving instinct
heckling, heckling instinct
hedonism, hedonism instinct
hedonistic, hedonistic-delight instinct
heeding, heeding instinct

heedlessness, heedlessness instinct

heliophobia, heliophobia (fear of the sun/sunlight) instinct

help, to-beg-for-help instinct

help, to-give-help-to-someone instinct (helping-behavior instinct)

help, to-help-a-person-in-distress instinct

help, you-shout-'help'-when-you-are-in-danger instinct

helpfulness, helpfulness instinct

helplessness, a-feeling-of-helplessness instinct

helplessness, an-expression-of-helplessness instinct

hematophobia, hematophobia (fear of the sight of blood/blood) instincts (also called hemophobia)

hemophobia, hemophobia (fear of the sight of blood/blood) instincts (also called hematophobia)

hen party, hen-party (a gathering at which only women are present) instinct

herd, herd instinct (gregariousness instinct)

heroism, heroism instinct

hesitancy, hesitancy instinct

hesitation, hesitation instinct

heterosexuality, heterosexuality instinct

heuristic, heuristic-guided-look-ahead instinct

hide, to-hide-behind-their-mother's-skirts instinct

hide, to-hide-one's-feelings instinct

hide, to-hide-oneself instinct

hide, to-hide-something instinct

hidebound, people-are-hidebound instinct

hierarchy, social-hierarchy instinct(s) (see: Introduction)

hierophobia, hierophobia (fear of religion/sacred objects associated with religion/religious rites) instincts

high, the-'high'-that-many-runners-feel-during-and-right-after-endurance-runs instinct

high, to-feel-an-unpleasantly-high-temperature instinct

high, to-hold-one's-head-high instinct

high, your-spirits-are-high instinct high horse, to-be-on-one's-high-horse instinct

high places, dread-of-or-in-high-places instinct

high-risk, high-risk-behaviors instincts

high spirits, to-be-in-high-spirits instinct

hilarity, hilarity instinct

hit back, to-hit-back instinct

hoarding, hoarding instinct

hoarding, hoarding-is-taboo instinct

hoaxing, hoaxing instinct

hoggishness, hoggishness instinct

homage, homage instinct

home, a-basic-tendency-to-return-to-a-fixed-home-base instinct

home, home-building instinct

homesickness, homesickness instinct

homing, homing-ability instinct

homogamy, homogamy instinct (the tendency for people to select mates who are similar to themselves)

homophobia, homophobia (fear of homosexuality) instinct

homosexuality, homosexuality instinct

honest, to-be-basically-honest-and-reliable instinct

honesty, honesty instinct

honor, honor instinct

honor, personal-honor instinct

honor, the-defense-of-personal-honor instinct

honor, to-honor-someone instinct

hooliganism, hooliganism instinct

hoot, to-hoot-down-someone instinct

hope, hope (a feeling of desire and expectation) instinct

hopping, children's-hopping,-skipping,-throwing,-and-other-motor-behaviors instinct

horror, horror instinct

hospitality, hospitality instinct

hostages, frightened-hostages-often-develop-friendly-feelings-toward-their-captors instinct

hostile, hostile-infantile-signals instincts

hostility, deep,-irrational-hostility instinct

hostility, hostility instinct

hostility, hostility-to-an-idea instinct

hostility, our-occasional-hostility-toward-people-who-look-different-from-ourselves instinct

hotly, to-hotly-debate-a-topic instinct

how things work, to-like-knowing-how-things-work instinct

hubris, hubris instinct

hues, our-discrimination-of-hues instinct

humiliate, to-humiliate-someone instinct

humiliation, feeling-of-humiliation instinct

humility, humility instinct

humor, black-humor instinct

humor, crude-humor instinct

humor, grim-humor instinct (= sardonic-humor instinct)

humor, the-sense-of-humor instinct

humor, we-often-use-humor-to-deal-with-things-intensely-painful instinct

humor, when-oppressed-peoples-have-no-other-remedy-they-resort-to-humor instinct

hunger, the-feeling-of-hunger instinct

hungry, feeling-hungry-and-starting-to-eat instinct (normal behavior needs to be explained!)

hungry, to-feel-hungry instinct

hunt, the-excitement-of-the-hunt instinct

hunting, hunting-and-prey-killing instinct (Work has become the major substitute for primitive hunting. Sporting activities are modified forms of hunting behavior.)

hurt, to-feel-hurt instinct (= hurt-feelings instinct)

hurtful, to-say-hurtful-things instinct
hyalophobia, hyalophobia (fear of glass) instinct
hydrophobia, hydrophobia (fear of water) instinct
hygienic, hygienic-behavior instincts
hypergamy, hypergamy instinct (Hypergamy is the female practice of
marrying men of equal or greater wealth and status)
hyperthymia, hyperthymia (exaggerated emotional excitement) instinct
hypertrichophobia, hypertrichophobia (fear of growth of bodily hair,
particularly, excessive amounts) instinct
hypnophobia, hypnophobia (fear of falling asleep) instinct
hypnotic, hypnotic-suggestion instinct
hypocrisy, hypocrisy instinct
hypomania, hypomania (mild condition of overexcitability) instinct
hysterical, hysterical-laughter instinct

I

i, the-*i*-speech-sounds instinct (The *i* speech sounds are the minimal
units of instinctual speech sounds that correspond roughly to the letter *i*
of the alphabet)
iconicity, iconicity instinct
idea, to-get-an-idea instinct
idea, to-play-with-an-idea instinct
idealism, idealism instinct
idealization, idealization instinct
idealizing, idealizing instinct
ideas, intuitive-ideas instincts
ideation, ideation (the forming of ideas) instinct
identification, the-identification-of-individuals-by-voice-alone instinct
identify, a-mother-is-able-to-identify-her-baby-by-smell-alone instinct
identify, to-identify-with-someone-or-something instinct

identity, identity instincts

identity, self-identity instinct

ideomotor act, ideomotor-act (an overt act initiated by an idea) instinct

idiosyncracy, idiosyncracy instincts (all instincts are such instincts, more or less)

idleness, idleness instinct

idleness, idleness-is-contemptible-and-labor-is-honorable instinct

idolatry, idolatry instinct

idolizing, idolizing instinct

ignore, to-ignore-someone-or-something instinct

illicit, the-sense-of-illicit instinct

illusory, illusory-contour instinct

image, image-making instinct

imageless, imageless-thought instinct

imagery, pleasant-imagery instinct

imagery, visual-imagery instinct

imagination, imagination instinct

imagination, the-child's-imagination-is-very-active instincts

imitate, boys-are-more-likely-to-imitate-the-men,-and-girls-are-more-likely-to-imitate-the-women instinct

imitate, neonates-can-imitate-the-facial-expressions-of-adults instinct

imitation, imitation instinct

immobility, immobility instinct (death-feigning instinct)

immorality, immorality instincts

impatience, impatience instinct

imperious, to-be-imperious instinct

impertinence, impertinence instinct

impervious, to-be-impervious instinct

impetuosity, impetuosity instinct

impiety, impiety instinct

imploring, an-imploring-look instinct

imploring, imploring instinct

imposing, someone-or-something-is-imposing instinct

imprecation, imprecation instinct

impress, to-impress instinct

impress, you-impress-something-on-someone instinct

impressed, to-be-impressed-by-someone-or-something instinct

impression, to-get-an-impression instincts

impression, your-impression-of-a-person instinct

impression, your-impression-of-a-place instinct

impression, your-impression-of-a-situation instinct

impression, your-impression-of-a-thing instinct

imprinting, imprinting instincts (imprinting is learning; all instincts are learning instincts)

imprudence, imprudence (imprudent behavior or speech) instinct

impulsion, impulsion (a desire that you cannot control) instinct

impulsive, impulsive-behavior instinct (impulsiveness instinct)

impulsive, impulsive-violence instinct

impulsiveness, impulsiveness instinct

inadvertent, an-inadvertent-action instinct

inane, inane-remarks instinct

inattention, selective-inattention instincts

inbreeding, inbreeding-avoidance instincts

incest, incest-barrier instincts

incest, the-incest-avoidance instinct

incongruity, the-detection-of-incongruity instinct

incredulity, incredulity instinct

inculcate, you-inculcate-something-in-someone's-mind instinct

indebtedness, indebtedness instinct

indecision, indecision instinct

independent, to-like-being-independent instinct

indignant, indignant-dispute instinct

indignant, you-are-indignant instinct

indignation, indignation instinct

indignation, moral-indignation instinct

indignity, to-feel-indignity instinct

indoctrinability, indoctrinability instinct

indoctrination, indoctrination instinct

indolence, indolence (laziness) instinct

indolent, an-indolent-smile instinct

indomitable, an-indomitable-spirit instinct

induction, induction instinct

indulgence, indulgence instincts

infantile, infantile-play instinct

infatuation, infatuation instinct

inference, inference instincts

inferiority, inferiority-feeling instinct (= feelings-of-inferiority instinct)

infidelity, infidelity instinct

infidelity, our-anger-in-reaction-to-infidelity instinct

information, information-talking instinct

in-group, in-group-solidarity instinct

inhibition, inhibition instincts (e.g. signals that inhibit attacks within the social group)

inhibitions, our-inhibitions-about-killing-fellow-humans instinct

injustice, a-sense-of-injustice instinct

innovativeness, innovativeness instincts

inquisitive, to-be-inquisitive instinct (= inquisitiveness instinct)

insecurity, the-feelings-of-insecurity instinct

insecurity, we-cry-if-we-are-faced-with-a-high-degree-of-insecurity instinct

insensitivity, insensitivity-and-lack-of-tact instinct

insight, sudden-insight instincts (= a-burst-of-insight instincts)

insincerity, insincerity instinct

insinuation, insinuation instinct

insist, to-insist-on-something instinct

inspect, to-inspect-one's-environment-with-one's-eyes instinct

inspiration, inspiration instinct

inspirited, feeling-inspirited instinct

institutionalizing, institutionalizing-the-moral-values-of-the-community instinct

insularity, insularity instinct

insulting, insulting-gestures instincts

insulting, insulting-remark instinct

insulting, to-become-angry-at-an-insulting-person instinct

insult-signals, insult-signals instincts (disinterest signals, boredom signals, impatience signals, the tight smile, the cheek crease, mock-discomfort signals, dominant nose-in-air display, mockery signals, spitting aimed directly at the insulted person, pushing, flicking, flapping, swiping, holding the nose as if protecting oneself from a bad smell, obscene comments, a sneering, contorted face thrust close to our own, etc)

intellection, intellection (conception, comparison, abstraction, generalization, reasoning) instincts

intellectual, intellectual-fight instinct

intelligence, "everyday intelligence" instincts

intelligence, intelligence instincts (linguistic intelligence, mathematical intelligence, musical intelligence, visual-spatial intelligence, bodily intelligence, intrapersonal intelligence, interpersonal intelligence, emotional intelligence, etc)

intent, intent instincts

intention, intention instincts

intentionality, intentionality instincts

interest, interest-in-the-normal,-standard-activities-of-living instinct

interpreting, interpreting instincts

intimacy, the-feelings-of-intimacy instinct (the-need-for-intimacy instinct)

intimate, intimate-extended-cuddlings,-fondlings,-kissings,-strokings instinct

intimidate, to-intimidate-one-another instinct (= intimidating-behavior instinct)

intimidated, to-feel-intimidated instinct

intimidation, postures-of-intimidation instincts
intonation, intonation instincts
intrepidity, intrepidity instinct
intrigued, to-be-intrigued-by-something instinct
introspection, the-capacity-for-introspection instincts
introversion, introversion instinct
intuition, intuition instincts
intuition, intuition-based-on-emotion instincts
invariant, invariant-right instinct (The rule of the «invariant right» is a tendency to veer that way after entering a store. Even Brits who drive on the other side of the road obey the rule of the «invariant right»)
inventiveness, inventiveness instinct
investigation, investigation instincts
invigorated, to-feel-invigorated instinct
invocation, invocation instinct
iophobia, iophobia (fear of being poisoned/rusty objects) instincts
irascible, irascible-outbursts instincts
irony, irony instinct
irritability, irritability instinct
irritable, irritable-mood instinct
irritated, the-irritated-head-toss instinct
irritation, irritation instinct
irritations, sudden-scratchings-or-nibblings,-directed-at-specific-irritations instinct
isolation, a-sense-of-isolation instinct
itchy feeling, itchy-feeling instinct

J

j, the-*j*-speech-sounds instinct (The *j* speech sounds are the minimal units of instinctual speech sounds that correspond roughly to the letter *j* of the alphabet)

    jabber, to-jabber instinct
    jaded, to-get-jaded instinct
    jaundiced, a-jaundiced-attitude instinct
    jaw, jaw-dislocating instinct
    jealous, jealous-rage instinct
    jealousy, jealousy instinct
    jealousy, sexual-jealousy instinct
    jeer, to-jeer-at-someone instinct
    jerk out, to-jerk-out-a-remark-or-comment instinct
    jest, jest instinct
    jest, you-say-something-in-jest instinct
    jibe, jibe instinct
    jibe, the-sarcastic-jibe-of-hatred-and-insult instinct
    jingoism, jingoism instinct
    jitters, getting-the-jitters instinct
    jocularity, jocularity instinct
    joke, laugh-at-a-visual-or-verbal-joke instinct
    joke, to-joke-or-to-say-or-do-something-jokingly instinct
    jokes, to-share-acerbic-jokes instinct
    jollity, jollity instinct
    joviality, joviality instinct
    joy, joy instinct
    joy, joy-of-life instinct
    jubilation, jubilation instinct
    judge, judge-people-fairly-accurately-on-first-appearances instinct
    judgement, judgement-and-emotion-are-deeply-intertwined instinct

justice, justice instinct
justice, the-desire-for-social-justice instinct

K

k, the-*k*-speech-sounds instinct (The *k* speech sounds are the minimal units of instinctual speech sounds that correspond roughly to the letter *k* of the alphabet)

kainophobia, kainophobia (fear of new things/new experiences/new situations) instincts

keenness, keenness instinct

keeping your distance, keeping-your-distance (defending your personal space) instinct

kenophobia, kenophobia (fear of empty spaces) instinct

keraunophobia, keraunophobia (fear of lightning/thunder) instincts

kick, to-get-a-kick-from-something instinct

kick, to-kick-against-a-situation instinct

kid, to-kid-someone instinct

kid, to-kid-yourself instinct

kill, to-say-that-you-will-kill-someone instinct

kill prey, the-urge-to-kill-prey instinct (it keeps reappearing with startling regularity in the playful activities of young boys, but in the adult world it is subjected to powerful cultural suppression)

kindliness, kindliness instinct

kindness, kindness instinct

kindness, to-value-kindness instinct

kinesthetics, kinesthetics (feeling of motion) instincts

kinship, the-extent-and-formalization-of-kinship-ties instinct

kiss feeding, kiss-feeding (non-milk feeding) instincts (the mother's kiss-feeding instinct and the baby's kiss-feeding instinct). Mothers wean their children by chewing up their food and then passing it into the infantile mouth by lip-to-lip contact. Our species probably practiced it for a million years or more.

kissing, kissing instinct

kleptomania, kleptomania instinct

knocking, your-heart-is-knocking-with-fright instinct

knot, your-stomach-knots-because-you-are-afraid-or-excited instinct

knowing, a-knowing-look-instinct

knowing, feeling-of-knowing instinct

knowing, to-enjoy-knowing-how-things-work instinct

knowledge, love-of-knowledge instinct

knowledge, the-quest-for-knowledge instincts

kopophobia, kopophobia (fear of becoming fatigued or exhausted) instincts

L

l, the-*l*-speech-sounds instinct (The *l* speech sounds are the minimal units of instinctual speech sounds that correspond roughly to the letter *l* of the alphabet)

labor,   cooperatve-division-of-labor-between-adult-males-and-females instincts

lackey, lackey instinct

lalophobia, lalophobia (fear of speaking/stammering or committing errors while speaking) instincts

lament, you-lament-something instincts

lamentation, lamentation instinct

lamenting, lamenting-the-misfortune instinct

language, language instincts

language, language-perception instincts (Language perception is reflexive: fast, automatic, and innate, like reflexes)

languid, to-be-languid instinct

languishing, languishing instinct
languor, languor instinct
lash, to-lash-out-at-or-against-someone instinct
lash, to-lash-out-with-your-hands-or-with-a-weapon instinct
lassitude, lassitude instinct
laterality, laterality instincts
laugh, he-laughs-through-clenched-teeth-at-jokes-about-him instinct
laugh, the-baby's-laugh instinct
laugh, to-laugh-at-yourself instinct
laugh, to-laugh-out-loud instinct
laugh, to-laugh-to-scorn instinct
laugh, to-laugh-very-heartily instinct
laughing, laughing-at-someone instinct
laughter, an-uncontrollable-bout-of-laughter instinct
laughter, laughter-of-scorn instinct
laughter, the-contagiousness-of-laughter instinct
laughter, to-burst-into-laughter instinct
laxness, laxness instinct
lay the blame, to-lay-the-blame-on-someone-or-something instinct
laziness, laziness instinct
lead, to-take-the-lead-in-a-particular-situation-or-group instinct
leader, to-be-a-leader instinct
leaders, intense-attention-toward-leaders instinct
leading males, attention-structure-is-centripetal-on-leading-males instinct
league, league instinct
learning, learning instincts (Associative learning, ideational learning, learning without awareness, motor learning, observational learning, pattern learning (relational learning), perceptional learning, response learning (place learning), rote learning, stimulus-response learning, stimulus-stimulus learning, to learn from experience, trial-and-error learning, learning by imitation, "X always immediately preceded Y" learning, learning from the consequences of your behavior, "we can benefit from the

experiences of others" learning, insight learning, etc, are merely *learning situations*. Remember that only instincts can learn. *We don't have to learn to learn because we have learning instincts.*

leave, thoughts-leave-your-mind instinct

lechery, lechery instinct

leering, leering instinct

leering, leering-looks instinct

leisure, the-need-for-leisure instinct

lesbianism, lesbianism instinct

letdown, letdown instinct

lethargy, lethargy instinct

levity, levity instinct

levophobia, levophobia (fear of things being on the left side of one's body) instinct

lewdness, lewdness instinct

liberality, liberality instinct

lick, lick-one's-wounds instinct

lick, lick-our-lips instinct

licking, the-general-licking instinct

light, light-heartedness instinct

lighting, to-regard-objects-as-having-colors-independent-of-lighting instinct

liking, liking instinct

liking, liking-a-person instinct

limb, limb-movements instincts

limb, limb-position instincts

limp, if-you-step-on-a-thorn-you-know-that-you-need-to-limp instinct

lingering, the-lingering-feelings-for-a-lost-love instinct

lip, lip-eroticism instinct

lips, men-desire-women-with-full-lips-and-small-chins instinct

lips, to-bite-one's-lips instinct

listening, listening instinct

liveliness, liveliness instinct (= to-be-lively instinct)

loathing, loathing instinct

locality, locality-survey instinct

locating, locating-a-sound-source-in-the-environment instinct

locating, locating-a-stimulus-in-the-visual-field instinct

locating, locating-the-point-of-stimulation-on-the-skin instinct

location, to-expect-an-object-to-have-a-location,-even-when-it-is-not-presently-perceivable instinct

locomotion, a-striding,-bipedal-locomotion instinct

locomotion, locomotion instincts (the slither, the crawl, the totter, the walk, the stroll, the shuffle, the hurry, the run, the jog, the sprint, the tip-toe, the march, the goose-step, the jump, the hop, the skip, the climb, the swing, acrobatics, the baby's swimming)

logical, logical-reasoning instincts (= logical-thinking instincts)

loneliness, a-feeling-of-loneliness instinct

lonely, to-feel-lonely instinct

longing, longing (a rather sad feeling of wanting something very much) instinct

longing, longing-for-something instinct

look, look-hard-at-somebody instinct

look, to-be-too-ashamed-or-embarrassed-to-look-at-someone-directly instinct

look, we-prefer-to-look-at-patterned-stimuli-with-sharp-contours instinct

looking, looking-towards-the-sound instinct

looks, angry-looks instinct

looks, leering-looks instinct

looks, loving-looks instinct

looks, suspicious-looks instinct

looks, tender-looks instinct

looks, understanding-looks instinct

loquacity, loquacity instinct

losing, to-hate-losing instinct

lost, to-be-lost-in-thought,-a-thing,-etc instinct (e.g. to become «lost» in a beautiful sunset)

loud, loud-and-intrusive-noises-irritate-and-annoy-you instinct

loudly, to-speak-loudly-and-angrily instinct

lounge, to-lounge-about(-or-lounge-around) instinct

lousy, to-feel-lousy intinct

love, a-kid-needs-love instinct

love, love-at-first-sight instinct

love, love-bites instinct

love, love-nibble instinct

love, parental-love instinct

love, to-be-in-love instinct

love, to-be-in-love-with-being-in-love instinct

love, to-fall-out-of-love instinct

lovers, lovers'-baby-talk instinct

loving, the-love-of-loving instinct

lowering, the-lowering-of-the-body-in-relation-to-the-dominant-individual instinct (e.g. groveling, prostrating, kneeling, bowing, curtsying)

loyalty, loyalty-in-fighting instinct

loyalty, loyalty-on-the-hunt (or work) instinct

loyalty, loyalty-to-duty instinct

lubrication, vaginal-lubrication instinct

lubricity, lubricity instinct

ludicrous, you-describe-someone-or-something-as-ludicrous instinct

lying, lying instinct

lynch, lynch-mobs instinct (remember: all instincts are situational!)

lyricism, lyricism instinct

M

m, the-*m*-speech-sounds instinct (The *m* speech sounds are the minimal units of instinctual speech sounds that correspond roughly to the letter *m* of the alphabet)

machismo, machismo instinct

macrophobia, macrophobia (fear of large objects) instinct

magnanimity, magnanimity instinct

magnetic, magnetic-compass instinct

main meals, main-meals instinct

maintain, ability-to-maintain-concentrated-attention instinct

make up, to-make-up-your-mind-about-something instinct

malaise, malaise (slight bodily discomfort) instinct

male chauvinism, male-chauvinism instinct

male-grouping, the-male-grouping-hunting-tendency-of-our-species instinct

male status, male-status instinct

male violence, male-violence instinct

maleness, maleness instincts

malevolence, malevolence instinct

malice, malice instinct

malignancy, malignancy instinct

malleability, malleability instinct

mammalingus, mammalingus instinct

mania, mania instincts. Manias are abnormal instincts. There are an enormous number of manias

manipulate, to-manipulate,-handle-and-explore-objects instinct

manipulate, to-manipulate-others-through-violence-and-reconciliation instinct

manipulation, psychological-manipulation instinct

manipulation, resisting-psychological-manipulation-instinct

map, a-mental-map-of-reality instincts
masculinity, masculinity instinct
masochism, masochism instinct
mass-contagion (fads, fashions, dress styles, political movements, etc.) instinct
mass suggestion, mass-suggestion instinct
massacre, massacre instinct (remember: instincts are situational)
mastering, the-pleasure-of-mastering-something-new instinct
masticating, masticating instinct
masturbation, masturbation instinct
masturbation, masturbation-fantasies instinct
mate, mate-for-life instinct (Nine out of ten mammals that mate for life are unfaithful. Man is *not* genetically monogamous. Only two primates are genetically monogamous: the marmoset and the tamarin. Research suggests left-handed people (like Bill Clinton) are more prone to compulsive sex addiction.)
mate, mate-selection instincts
mate, the-qualities-man-prefers-in-a-mate:-Men-pay-more-attention-to-youth-and-beauty,-women-to-wealth-and-status instincts
matechoice, matechoice instincts (mate choice reveals a distinct gender gap)
matechoice copying, matechoice-copying instinct (women are more likely to express an interest in going out with a man if they are told that other women also find him attractive)
maternal, maternal instincts
maternal, maternal-care instincts
maternal mood, the-baby-is-acutely-responsive-to-maternal-mood instinct
mathematical, mathematical-intuition instincts (an-intuitive-grasp-of-mathematics,-even-of-mathematical-theorems instincts)
mathematical, mathematical-reasoning instincts
maudlin, to-become-maudlin instinct
mawkish, a-mawkish-pride instinct

mawkishness, mawkishness instinct

mayhem, mayhem instincts

meals, main-meals instinct

mealtimes, mealtimes instinct

meaning, finding-meaning instinct

meaningfulness, a-feeling-of-meaningfulness instinct

meaninglessness, a-feeling-of-meaninglessness

meat, the-urge-to-eat-meat instinct (our old primate omnivory)

mechanical, mechanical-ability instincts

meddle, to-meddle-in-something instinct

medical, medical-care instinct (Woolly monkeys can diagnose their own illnesses and choose to eat plants that provide the perfect cures. When you send them away to another country with its own set of plant life, the woolly monkeys adapt. Instincts are situational!

meditation, meditation instinct

meekness, meekness instinct

melancholy, melancholy instinct

melodramatic, melodramatic-behavior instinct

melody, melody instinct

memories, retrieval-of-long-term-memories instinct

memories, retrieval-of-short-term-memories instinct

memories, the-formation-of-new-memories instincts

memorization, rote-memorization-of-details instinct

memory, auditory-sensory-memory instinct

memory, declarative-memory instinct (= semantic and episodic memory)

memory, eidetic-images-memory instinct

memory, emotional-memory instinct

memory, episodic-memory instinct (= memory for information about specific experiences)

memory, flashbulb-memories instinct

memory, location-memory instinct

memory, long-term-memory instinct

memory, memory-consolidation-during-REM-sleep instinct

memory, memory-for-words instinct

memory, motor-memory instincts

memory, musical-memory instinct

memory, object-memory instinct

memory, olfactory-memory instinct

memory, procedural-memory instinct (= memory for motor movements, skills, and other procedures)

memory, semantic-memory instinct (= memory for meaning)

memory, visual-memory instinct

mental set, mental-set instincts (= a habitual way of approaching or perceiving a problem)

mercy, mercy instinct

merriment, merriment instinct

merry, to-make-merry-with-friends instinct

meticulousness, meticulousness instinct

microphobia, microphobia (fear of small objects) instinct

microsynchrony,   microsynchrony-of-small-movements-when-a-pair-of-friends-are-in-a-condition-of-strong-rapport instinct

militancy, militancy instinct

mime, mime instinct

mimicry, mimicry instinct

mince, you-do-not-mince-your-words instinct

mince, you-mince-your-way-somewhere instinct

mind, the-ability-to-form-a-theory-of-mind-about-another-person instinct

miracle, to-treat-as-a-miracle instinct

mirth, mirth instinct

miser, miser instinct

miserable, to-be-made-miserable-by-your-mistakes instinct

miserable, to-feel-miserable instinct

misgivings, you-have-misgivings-about-something instinct

miss, you-miss-someone instinct

missing, the-feeling-of-missing-the-loved-one instinct

missionary, missionary-enthusiasm instinct

moaning, moaning instinct

mob, bloodthirsty-lynch-mob instinct

mob, to-mob-someone instinct (There are cases daily in schools round about of pupils being mobbed by fellow pupils. Also adults and animals mob.)

mock, mock-aggression instinct

mock, mock-fight instinct

mock, to-mock-a-person-or-something-that-they-do instinct

mocking, mocking instinct

model, to-model-yourself-on-someone instinct

moderate polygyny, moderate-polygyny instinct (We are moderately polygynous. About three-fourths of all human societies permit the taking of multiple wives, and most of them encourage the practice by law and custom. The monogamous societies fit that category in a legal sense only.)

moderation, moderation instinct (moderate-behavior instinct)

modesty, modesty instinct

modesty, to-value-modesty instinct

monophobia, monophobia (fear of being left alone) instinct

monopolize, males-monopolize-their-mates,-and-vice-versa instinct

mood, bad-mood instincts

mood, good-mood instincts

mood, lousy-mood instincts

mood, mood instincts

mood, mood-talking instincts (e.g. the words 'I am hurt' are whined or screamed, the words 'I am furious' are roared or bellowed)

mood, to-feel-the-mood-of-others instinct (to-sense-people's-moods instinct)

mood, you-are-*in-no-mood*-for-something instincts

mood, you-are-*in-the-mood*-for-something instincts

moodiness, moodiness instinct

moral, a-moral-sense instinct

moral, to-construct-a-moral-order instincts

moral, tribal-moral-codes instincts

morally, to-feel-morally-responsible instinct

morbid, to-be-morbid instinct

mordant, mordant-humor instinct

morose, a-morose-facial-expression instinct

morphemes, morphemes instincts (morphemes are the smallest units of meaning in a language)

mortification, mortification instinct

mortified, to-be-mortified instinct

motherese, motherese (the speech of adults to young children) instinct

mothers, mothers-feel-attachment-to-their-newborn-babies instinct (mothers who feel no attachment to their newborn babies may lack a neural pathway that is normally triggered by the act of giving birth, a new study of mice suggests)

motion, motion instincts (see locomotion instincts)

motion, to-perceive-motion-as-continuous instinct (Although our visual perceptions of objects are discrete because of our saccadic movements, we perceive objects as moving continuously. Perceiving motion as continuous may have evolved very early among vertebrates.)

motionless, motionless-postures instincts

motivated, motivated-forgetting instinct

motor, involuntary-motor-movements instincts

motor, motor-control instincts

motor, motor-coordination instincts

motor, voluntary-motor-movements instincts

mourning, mourning instinct

mouth, orienting-the-mouth instinct

moved, being-moved instinct

moved, to-be-moved-by-music instinct

movements, the-involuntary-movements-of-the-limbs-and-body instincts

movements, the-voluntary-movements-of-the-limbs-and-body instincts

mugging, mugging instinct
mumbling, mumbling instinct
murder, our-inhibitions-against-murder instinct
murmuring, murmuring instinct
muscle, maintaining-muscle-tone-and-muscular-coordination instincts
muscle, muscle-eroticism (pleasure in bodily activity) instinct
muscle, muscle sensation,
muse, to-muse-about-something instinct
musement, musement instinct
musement, the-play-of-musement instinct
music, music instinct
music, our-love-of-music instinct
musical, musical-ear instinct
musical, musical-harmony instinct
musical, musical-melody instinct
musical, musical-scale instinct
muster, to-muster-all-your-self-control instinct
muster, to-muster-up-your-courage instinct
mute, you-mute-your-feelings,-emotions,-or activities instincts
muttering, muttering instinct
muttering, muttering-to-himself/herself instinct
mysophobia, mysophobia (fear of dirt/contamination) instincts
mystique, an-atmosphere-of-mystique instinct

N

n, the-*n*-speech-sounds instinct (The *n* speech sounds are the minimal units of instinctual speech sounds that correspond roughly to the letter *n* of the alphabet)
nagging, a-doubt-is-nagging-at-you instinct
nagging, a-worry-is-nagging-at-you instinct

naked, photographs-of-naked-or-almost-naked-women-in-a-way-which-is-intended-to-please-men,-is-offensive-to-many-women instinct

name, name-calling instinct

name, to-give-someone/something-a-name,-and-call-someone/something-by-this-name-afterwards instinct (naming instinct)

names, infants-respond-positively-to-the-sound-of-their-names instinct

nap, nap instinct

narcissism, narcissism instinct

nastiness, nastiness instinct

nationalism, nationalism instinct

natter, to-natter instinct

natural kinds, we-are-predisposed-to-name-kinds-of-entities-and-to-expect-that-the-objects-of-a-kind-that-is-recognized-by-superficial-properties-will-have-additional-properties-in-common instinct

nature, our-love-for-nature instinct (biophilia instinct)

nature, to-enjoy-beautiful-nature instinct

nature, to-feel-at-one-with-nature instinct

naughtiness, to-enjoy-stories-about-naughtiness instinct

nausea, nausea instinct

navigation, men-generally-navigate-paths-by-pure-guesses-of-relative-distances-and-angles instinct

navigation, the-general-navigation instinct

navigation, women-generally-navigate-paths-by-recognizing-particular-landmarks instinct

nearing, nearing-a-baby instinct

neat, a-feeling-that-something-is-neat instinct

neat, to-be-neat-and-tidy instinct

necking, necking (kissing each other passionately) instinct

necrophilia, necrophilia instinct (an abnormal instinct indeed)

necrophobia, necrophobia (fear of death/dead things/dead human corpses) instincts

negative, negative-self-feeling instinct (remember: instincts are situational) negotiation, negotiation instinct

neophilia, neophilia (a desire for the new and novel and/or a tendency to try new foods) instincts

neophobia, neophobia (fear of the new/the novel/new foods) instincts (If we lost our neophilia, we would stagnate. If we lost our neophobia, we would rush headlong into disaster)

nepotism, nepotism instinct

nervous, nervous-anticipation instinct

nervous, nervous-excitement instinct

nervous, nervous-panic instinct

nervous, nervous-tension instinct

nervousness, nervousness instinct

neutral, neutral-voice instinct

new, the-fear-of-the-new instinct

new, the-pleasure-of-mastering-something-new instinct

new, the-urge-to-investigate-the-new-and-the-novel instinct

new, to-like-learning-new-things instinct

new, to-like-looking-at-new-things instinct

news, to-ask-for-news-of-mutual-acquaintances instinct

nibblings, minor-nibblings-between-our-main-meals instinct

nice, people-tend-to-be-nice-to-those-who-are-nice-to-them instinct

nice-looking, a-feeling-that-someone-is-nice-looking instinct

nicknaming, nicknaming instinct (= naming instinct)

niggle, niggle (a small worry or doubt that you keep thinking about) instinct

nightmares, to-get-nightmares instinct

nihilism, nihilism instinct

nits, picking-nits instinct

no, a-wagging-forefinger-for-'no' instinct

no, the-head-shake-for-'no' instinct

nobleness, nobleness instinct

nocturnal, nocturnal-orgasm instinct

nodding, nodding-and-smiling-in-the-private-conversation instinct

noise, newborns-are-easily-perturbed-by-noise-and-movement instinct

noise, noise-rejection instinct (Certain appearances are «noise», e.g. shadows. We are predisposed to regard shadows as «noise» and to ignore the edges of shadows.)

noises, noises-irritate-and-annoy-you instinct

nonchalance, nonchalance instinct

non-conformity, non-conformity instinct

non-verbal, non-verbal-communication (prosody, vocal paralanguage, non-vocal paralanguage, etc) instincts

non-violence, non-violence instinct

non-vocal, non-vocal-paralanguage (body postures, motion, touch, facial expressions, chemical communication, etc) instincts

normal mood, normal-mood (tranquility, a pleasant relaxed state) instinct

nose, orienting-the-nose instinct

nosiness, nosiness instinct

nosism, nosism instinct

nosophobia, nosophobia (fear of illness/acquiring some specific illness) instincts

nostalgia, nostalgia instinct

note, note (a particular quality in someone's voice that shows how they are feeling) instincts (e.g. a note of uncertainty)

notion, notion instinct

novelty, novelty-seeking instinct

novelty, the-need-for-novelty-and-excitement instinct

nude, males-are-sexually-aroused-by-watching-(photographs-that-display-)the-nude-body-of-a-member-of-the-opposite-sex instinct

nude, women-are-less-excited-by-(the-image-of-)anonymous-nude-males instinct

nudge, to-nudge-someone-into-doing-something instinct

number, the-number-sense instinct (People have lost their number sense as a result of brain damage. Many nonhuman animals have been shown experimentally to have a number sense.)

numbing, psychological-numbing (a reaction of surviving victims) instinct

numinous, numinous-perception instinct

nurse, nurse-your-grief,-anger-and-discontent-deep-inside-you instinct

nursing, nursing instinct

nursing, nursing-your-pride instinct

nurturance, nurturance instinct

nurturant, women-are-more-nurturant-than-men instinct

nurture, nurture instinct

nurturing, to-be-nurturing instinct

nuzzle, to-nuzzle-someone-or-something instinct

nyctophobia, nyctophobia (fear of night/the dark/darkness) instincts

nymphomania, nymphomania instinct

O

o, the-*o*-speech-sounds instinct (The *o* speech sounds are the minimal units of instinctual speech sounds that correspond roughly to the letter *o* of the alphabet)

obduracy, obduracy instinct

obedience, obedience-to-authority instinct

obeisance, the-obeisance-of-subordinates instinct

obey, the-tendency-to-obey-social-rules-and-laws instinct

obeying, obeying-orders instinct

obfuscation, obfuscation instinct

object, object-directedness instincts

object, object-permanence instinct

objection, objection instinct

objects, the-ability-to-distinguish-objects instinct

objects, the-infant-takes-great-pleasure-in-pushing,-pulling,-and-mouthing-objects intincts

objects, to-assume-that-objects-are-solid-and-therefore-two-objects-can-not-occupy-the-same-space-at-the-same-time instinct

objects, to-examine-and-manipulate-objects instincts

objects, to-identify-objects instinct (to-identify-a-part-of-the-current-stimulus-pattern-as-coming-from-an-object instinct)

obligated, to-feel-obligated-to-do-something instinct

obscene, being-obscene instinct (obscenity instinct)

obscene, obscene-signals instincts

obsequiousness, obsequiousness instinct

observation, observation instinct

obsession, obsession instincts. Obsessions are abnormal instincts

obsession, obsession-compulsion-control instincts

obsessiveness, obsessiveness instincts

obstinacy, obstinacy instinct

ochlophobia, ochlophobia (fear of crowds/crowded places) instincts

odium, odium instinct

odontophobia, odontophobia (fear of teeth/having one's teeth worked on by a dentist) instincts

odor, falling-in-love-involves-a-kind-of-fixation-on-the-specific-individual-odor-of-the-partner's-body instinct

odor, odor instincts (seven primary odors are assumed: camphorous, musky, floral, minty, ethereal, pungent, putrid)

odor preferences, before-puberty-there-are-preferences-for-sweet-and-fruity-odors instinct

odor preferences, from-puberty-there-are-preferences-for-flowery,-oily-and-musky-odors instinct

odor stimuli, certain-odor-stimuli-play-a-sexual-role instincts

odors, seven-primary-odors instincts (resinous, floral, minty, ethereal, musky, acrid, putrid)

off-key, music-is-off-key instinct

offences, to-attack-offences instinct

offend, to-offend-someone instinct

offended, to-be-offended instinct

oh, 'oh' instinct (a response or a comment on something that has just been said)

olfaction, olfaction (the sense of smell) instincts

olfactory, olfactory-eroticism (sexually exciting sensations associated with the sense of smell) instinct

ombrophobia, ombrophobia (fear of rainstorms) instinct

one-upmanship, one-upmanship instinct

onomatophobia, onomatophobia (fear of a particular word or name) instinct

onomatopoeia, onomatopoeia instinct

ooh, 'ooh' instinct (people say ooh when they are surprised, etc)

oops, 'oops' instinct (people say oops to indicate a mistake, etc)

open spaces, dread-in,-and-of,-open-spaces instinct

open, to-open-one's-mouth-in-order-to-express-surprise-or-shock instinct

openness, openness instinct

openness, openness-to-experience instinct

openness, openness-to-feelings instinct

operant conditioning, Note: (general) operant conditioning doesn't exist because learning is always specialized and content-dependent. All instincts are learning instincts, and only instincts can learn.

ophidiophobia, ophidiophobia (fear of snakes) instinct

opinion, to-have-a-high/low-opinion-of-someone instinct

opinions, get-cross-at-opinions-expressed-by-others instinct

opinions, opinions-are-difficult-to-shake instinct

opportunism, opportunism instinct

opposites, "opposites attract" instinct

opposition, opposition instinct

oppression, oppression instinct

optimism instinct

oral, oral-drive instinct
oral, oral-eroticism instinct
oral, oral-sadism (the desire to inflict pain through oral means) instinct
order, order instinct
order, to-order-someone-to-do-something (e.g. 'Sit down!') instinct
order, you-order-someone-to-do-something instinct (normal behavior needs to be explained)
orderliness, orderliness instinct
orders, obeying-orders instinct
organ, organ-eroticism instinct
organizing, organizing instinct (= organization instinct)
orgasm, nocturnal-orgasm instinct
orgasm, orgasm instinct
orientation, orientation instinct
orienting, orienting-response instinct
orienting, orienting-the-nose instinct
orthodoxy, orthodoxy instinct
orthography, orthography instincts (making-words instincts)
ostentation, ostentation instinct
ostracizing, ostracizing-someone instinct
other, a-sensitivity-to-the-feelings-of-other-people instinct
ouch, 'Ouch!' instinct (expressing sudden pain)
ouch, the-"ouch"-part-of-the-experience-of-pain instinct
out, to-feel-out-of-it instinct
outcry, outcry instinct
outlet, subsidiary-outlet-for-emotional-feelings instinct
outpourings, outpourings instinct
outrage, outrage instinct
outspokenness, outspokenness instinct
ovation, ovation instinct
overawed, to-be-overawed-by-someone-or-something instinct
overcompensation, overcompensation instinct

overconfidence, overconfidence instinct (a version of an instinct)
overreaction, overreaction instinct
ow, 'Ow!' instinct (people say 'Ow!' when they suddenly feel a pain)
ownership, ownership instinct (even Karl Marx had this particular instinct)
ownership, the-rituals-of-property-ownership instincts
ownership, to-gain-and-hold-ownership-over-things instinct

P

p, the-*p*-speech-sounds instinct (The *p* speech sounds are the minimal units of instinctual speech sounds that correspond roughly to the letter *p* of the alphabet)
pain, avoiding-pain instinct
pain, distressing-pain instinct
pain, psychological-pain instinct (Here: psychological = instinctual !!)
pain, the-emotional-and-behavioral-aspects-of-pain-sensations instincts
pain, to-feel-pain instinct (= the-feeling-of-pain instinct)
pain, to-show-strength-in-the-face-of-pain instinct
pained, a-puckered,-pained-expression instinct
pair bonding, pair-bonding instincts
palavering, palavering instinct
palm, to-palm-someone-off-with-an-excuse-or-a-lie instinct
palmar response, palmar-response instinct
palpitation, palpitation instinct
panache, panache instinct
panic, a-feeling-of-panic instinct
panic, a-surge-of-panic-instinct
panic, nervous-panic instinct
panic, panic-attack instinct
panic, the-panic-face instinct

pan(t)ophobia, pan(t)ophobia (fear of everything) instinct (a most unpleasant abnormal instinct)

parental, parental-affection instinct

parental, parental-care instinct

parental, parental-control-and-restraint instinct

parental, parental-devotion instinct

parental, parental-games instincts (peek-a-boo, hand-clapping, rhythmical knee-dropping, lifting high, tickling, play-hiding, play-fleeing, play-catching, etc.)

parental, parental-love instinct

parents, parents-smile-softly-at-the-baby instinct

parochialism, parochialism instinct

parsimony, devotion-to-parsimony instinct (= parsimony instinct)

part, to-take-someone's-part instinct

partiality, partiality instinct

parting, smiling-at-the-parting instinct

partition, partition-other-people-into-friends-and-aliens instinct

partners, how-we-attract-partners instincts

partners, women-choose-partners-from-a-wish-to-have-healthy-children instinct

parts, to-recognize-parts-of-an-object-and-their-relations-to-the-others instinct

parturiphobia, parturiphobia (fear of childbirth) instinct

party, party (social event) instinct

pass down, to-pass-down-stories,-traditions,-etc-to-a-younger-generation instinct

passion, a-feeling-of-very-strong-sexual-attraction-for-someone instinct

passion, a-passion-for-something/someone instinct

passion, passion (violent emotional outbreak) instinct

passionate, to-be-passionate-about-something instincts

passive, passive-resistance instinct

passive, passive-submission instinct

passiveness, passiveness instinct

pat, to-give-someone-a-pat-on-the-back (you tell them that you approve of what they have done or are trying to do) instinct

paternal, paternal instincts

pathos, pathos instinct

patience, patience instinct

patient, patient-tolerance instinct

patriotism, patriotism instinct

patrolling, patrolling-the-natural-environment instinct

pattern, pattern-detection instincts

pattern, pattern-discrimination instincts

pattern, pattern-recognition instincts

patterns, to-wish-to-discover-beautiful-patterns instinct

pay, to-pay-someone-back-for-doing-something-unpleasant-to-you instinct

peace, a-feeling-of-peace instinct

peace, peace-with-yourself instinct

peacemaking, peacemaking instinct

peccatophobia, peccatophobia (fear of committing a sin) instinct

peck, to-peck-someone-on-the-cheek (you give them a quick, light kiss) instinct

pecking order, pecking-order instincts

peckish, feeling-peckish instinct

peculiar, feeling-peculiar instincts

peculiar, seeing-blood-make-you-feel-a-bit-peculiar-inside-you instinct

pedantry, pedantry instinct

peddle, to-peddle-an-idea-or-information instinct

pedestal, to-knock-someone-off-their-pedestal instinct

pedestal, to-put-someone-on-a-pedestal instinct

pedophilia, pedophilia instinct (is an abnormal instinct)

peep, to-peep-at-something instinct

peer, peer-rejection instinct

peering, peering instinct

pelt, to-pelt-someone-with-something instinct

penal, penal-sanctions instinct

penance, penance instinct

penitence, penitence instinct

pep talk, pep-talk instinct

perception, perception instincts (visual perception, perception of time, etc)

perception, person-perception instinct

perception, self-perception instinct

perceptions, our-perceptions-are-influenced-by-our-emotions instincts

perceptual, perceptual-constancy instincts (brightness constancy, color constancy, size constancy, shape constancy)

perceptual, perceptual-integration instincts

perceptual, perceptual-process instincts. Perceptual processes are similar to reflexes. They are also fast, automatic, and innately specified, like reflexes. Remember that reflexes and instincts can learn

perfect pitch, to-have-perfect-pitch instinct

perfectionism, perfectionism instinct

permanence, object-permanence instinct

permissiveness, permissiveness instinct

perplexed, to-be-perplexed instinct

persecution, persecution instincts

perseverance, belief-perseverance instinct

perseverance, perseverance instinct

persistence, persistence instinct

persistent objects, to-expect-that-persistent-objects-exist instinct (having this prejudice is fundamental to the survival of humans and other land vertebrates)

person, person-perception instinct

personal attack, personal-attack instinct

personal identity, personal-identity (feeling of being the same person) instinct personal mark, the-need-to-leave-personal-mark-in-your-home-territory instinct

personal sincerity, personal-sincerity instinct (= that a man deal honestly with himself)

personal space, defending-your-personal-space instinct

personal space, personal-space instinct

personal territory, personal-territory instinct

personal vanity, personal-vanity-and-pride instinct

personhood, feeling-of-personhood instinct

perspective, a-sense-of-perspective instinct

persuade, to-persuade instinct (normal behavior needs to be explained!)

persuaded, to-be-persuaded instinct (normal behavior needs to be explained!)

persuasion, persuasion instinct (= to-persuade instinct)

persuasion, wheedling-persuasion instinct

perversity, perversity instincts. Perversities are abnormal instincts. There are an enormous number of perversities

pessimism, pessimism instinct

pestering, pestering instinct

pet, pet-idea instinct

pet, pet-name instinct

pettiness, pettiness instinct

petting, petting instinct

petulance, petulance instinct

phasmophobia, phasmophobia (fear of ghosts) instinct

pheromones, excreting-pheromones instincts

pheromones, reaction-to-pheromones instincts

phi, phi-phenomenon instinct

philanderer, philanderer instinct

philanthropy, philanthropy instinct

philia, philia instincts. Philias are abnormal instincts. There are an enormous number of philias

phlegmaticism, phlegmaticism (emotional coldness) instinct

phobophobia, phobophobia (fear of fear/acquiring a phobia) instincts

phoneme, phoneme-formation instincts (The English language has 44 phonemes)

phonemes, basic-phonemes instincts

phonophobia, phonophobia (fear of sound/the sound of one's own voice) instincts

physical attack, physical-attack intinct

physical attractiveness, the-sense-of-physical-attractiveness instinct

physical pain, the-emotional-and-bahavioral-aspects-of-the-feeling-of-physical-pain instinct

physical pain, we-cry-if-we-are-in-physical-pain instinct

physical strength, admiration-for-physical-strength-and-prowess instinct

pick a fight, to-pick-a-fight-or-quarrel-with-someone instinct

picking, picking-nits instinct

picking, picking-on-someone instinct

picture, to-picture-something-in-your-mind instinct

pictures, the-deriving-of-erotic-stimulation-from-viewing-sexually-oriented-pictures-or-films instinct

piety, piety instinct

pigheaded, to-be-pigheaded-and-determined instinct

piloerection, piloerection instinct

pilomotor, pilomotor-response ('goose-bumps') instinct

pine, to-be-pining-for-something instinct

pine, to-pine-for-someone-who-has-died-or-gone-away instinct

pique, pique instinct

pit, to-pit-your-wits-against-someone instinct

pitch, to-have-perfect-pitch instinct

pitifully, to-act-pitifully instinct

pitiless, pitiless instinct

pity, to-feel-pity-for-someone instinct

placate, to-placate-someone instinct

placidity, placidity instinct

plainspeaking, plainspeaking instinct

plaintive, a-plaintive-voice instinct

planning, planning instinct (= the-capacity-for-planned-action instinct)

platonic, platonic-friendship instinct

play, boys-play-more-with-"masculine"-toys instincts (genetic exceptions exist, e.g. most homosexuals)

play, girls-play-more-with-"feminine"-toys instincts (exceptions: e.g. tomboys (genetic!) and homosexuals (genetic, directly or indirectly))

play, play instincts (thrill play, muscle play, love-play (in the broadest sense), mechanical play, fantasy play, day-dreaming, clever play, creative play, locomotory play, vertigo play, neophilic play, play-fighting, play-chasing, play-fleeing, etc)

play, play-fighting instinct

play, play-talking instinct

play, rough-and-tumble-play instinct

play, the-mother/father-plays-with-her/his-baby instinct (making funny faces at the baby, tickling the baby, swinging the baby playfully up into the air, playing peekaboo, play-fleeing, play-hiding, play-discovering, pretending to drop the baby, etc)

play, the-play-face instinct

play, to-play-a-joke-or-a-trick-on-someone instinct

play, to-play-aggressively instinct

play, to-play-around-with-the-idea-of-doing-something instinct

playfulness, playfulness instinct (= a-sense-of-playfulness instinct)

plea, plea instinct

pleading, pleading instinct

pleasant, pleasant-imagery instinct

pleasantness, pleasantness instinct

pleasantry, pleasantry instinct

please others, to-please-others instinct

pleasure, pleasure instinct

pleasure, pleasure-hunting instinct
pleasure, providing-pleasure instinct
pleasure, vengeful-pleasure instinct
pleasure, we-experience-pleasure-in-our-daily-lives instincts
pleasures, general-interest-in-the-pleasures-of-life instinct
plod, to-plod-along instinct
pluck, to-pluck-up-the-courage-to-do-something instinct
plug away, to-plug-away-at-something instinct
plume on, to-plume-oneself-on-something instinct
plunge, to-plunge-into-an-activity instinct
poignancy, poignancy instinct
pointing, pointing instincts (the forefinger point, the hand point, the head point, the body point, the secretive eyes point, etc.)
poise, poise instinct
poison, to-poison-one's-mind-against-another-person instinct
poker face, poker-face instinct
polarizing, a-polarizing-opinion instincts
polemics, polemics instinct
politeness, politeness instinct
political, political-attack instinct
political, to-play-political-games instincts
polygynous, mildly-polygynous instinct
pomposity, pomposity instinct
ponder, to-ponder instinct
pong, pong (an unpleasant smell) instinct
ponophobia, ponophobia (fear of pain/work/being overworked) instincts
pooh, 'Pooh!' instinct (expressing disapproval or scorn)
position, to-keep-track-of-the-position-of-the-head-relative-to-the-stimulus-after-the-light-goes-out instinct
positive, positive-self-feeling instinct
possession, possession instinct
possessiveness, possessiveness-about-things instinct

possessiveness, possessiveness-towards-persons instinct

postural, postural-movements-associated-with-the-senses instincts

posture, posture instincts

posture, to-maintain-an-upright-posture instinct

pounds, your-heart-pounds-with-joy instinct

pouting, pouting-mouth instinct

power, power-assertion instinct

power, power-play instincts

power, power-struggle-for-dominance-within-the-group instinct

power, thirst-for-power instinct (= the-desire-for-power instinct)

power, will-to-power instinct

powerlessness, a-feeling-of-powerlessness instinct

practical, practical-joke instinct

practical, practical-reasoning instinct

practical, practical-understandings-of-things instincts

pragmatism, pragmatism instinct

praise, to-praise-someone-or-something instinct

prance, prance instinct

praying, praying-to-God instinct (also atheists and agnostics pray to God when reality steps in; instincts are situational)

preattentive, preattentive-processing instinct

precaution, precaution instincts

precious, precious-memories instinct

precious, precious-possessions instinct

precognition, precognition instinct

precoital, precoital-behaviors instincts

preconceived, preconceived-feelings instincts

preconception, preconception instincts

predators, escaping-from-predators instinct

prediction, prediction instincts

predictions, to-make-predictions-about-what-other-people-are-thinking instinct

preening, preening instinct
pregnancy, pregnancy-sickness instinct
prejudice, group-prejudice instincts
prejudice, prejudice instincts
preludes, dance-and-music-and-poetry-are-common-preludes-to-sex instincts
premeditation, premeditation instinct
premonition, premonition instinct
preoccupation, preoccupation instinct
preparedness, preparedness instincts
preparing, preparing-the-body-for-violent-activity instincts
presence, to-feel-another-person's-presence-in-the-room instinct
present, the-sense-of-the-present instinct
presentiment, presentiment instinct (foreboding instinct)
preservation, self-preservation instinct(s) (see: Introduction)
pressure sensation, the-emotional-and-behavioral-aspects-of-the-pressure-sensation instinct
pressure, the-pressure-of-too-great-expectation instinct
pressure, the-skin-is-sensitive-to-pressure instinct
prestige, prestige instinct
prestige, social-prestige instinct
presumption, presumption instinct
pretence, pretence instinct
pretension, pretension instinct
pride, ethnic-and-national-pride instinct
pride, nursing-your-pride instinct
pride, pride (a sense of dignity and self-respect) instinct
pride, to-have-pride-in-something-that-you-have instinct
pride, to-take-pride-in-something-that-you-do instinct
primacy, the-primacy-effect instinct (= early-presented information has an undue influence on final judgement)

principle of mediocrity, principle-of-mediocrity instinct (we can learn about our own capabilities from observing others, and we can learn about others by putting ourselves in their places)

privacy, the-sense-of-privacy instincts

privacy, the-sense-of-privacy-that-surround-sexual-feelings instinct

private, human-sex-is-a-private thing instinct

problem, problem-solving-activity instinct

problem, problem-solving-strategies instincts (trial-and-error reasoning, algorithmic reasoning, heuristic reasoning, logical reasoning)

problems, to-enjoy-solving-problems instinct

procedural, procedural-memory instinct (= memory for motor movements, skills, and other procedures)

prodding, prodding instinct

profanity, profanity instinct

promiscuity, promiscuity instinct (30 per cent of all white males have a gene for promiscuity. Human males in general have a tendency towards promiscuity, and females a tendency towards monogamy, as we would predict on evolutionary grounds.)

promise, to-promise-that-you-will-do-something instinct

proneness, proneness instinct

pronunciation, pronunciation instincts

propensity, propensity instinct

property, personal-property-and-space instincts

property, property instinct

property, property-rights instincts

property, we-tend-to-fight-tenaciously-for-property-which-we-have-put-great-effort-into-acquiring instinct

propitiation, propitiation instinct

proportion, rules-of-proportion-and-composition instincts

proprietarily, to-behave-proprietarily-toward-your-mate instinct

proselytize, to-proselytize instinct

prosody, prosody instincts (prosody = tone, tempo, rhythm, loudness, pacing, and other qualities of voice that modify the meaning of verbal utterances)
prostrate, you-prostrate-yourself instinct
prostrating, prostrating instinct
prostration, prostration instinct
protect, to-protect-your-territory instinct
protective, protective-feelings instincts
protective, to-feel-protective-of-a-baby-or-child instinct
protest, protest instinct
proud, to-feel-proud instinct
proudest, someone's-proudest-possession instinct
provocability, provocability instinct
provocability, the-victim's-provocability instinct
provocation, provocation instinct
prowess, admiration-for-physical-strength-and-prowess instinct
prowl, to-prowl instinct
proximity, the-principle-of-proximity instinct (the viewer perceives things that are close together as belonging together)
prudence, prudence instinct
prudery, prudery instinct
prudery, sexual-prudery instinct
prudishness, prudishness instinct
prurience, prurience instinct
pseudopresentiment, pseudopresentiment instinct
psychic pain, psychic-pain instinct
puckering, puckering instinct (= a-part-of-your-face-puckers instinct)
pugnacity, pugnacity instinct
pull, pull-oneself-together instinct
punctiliousness, punctiliousness instinct
punishment, punishment instinct

pupil, pupil-dilation/constriction-signals instincts (e.g. if a female/male feels emotionally attracted towards a male/female companion, her/his pupils dilate)

puppy, puppy-love instinct

purge, you-purge-your-thoughts-of-something-undesirable-such-as-hatred-or-envy instinct

purpose, a-sense-of-purpose instinct

purposive, purposive-activity instinct

purr, to-purr (speak in a soft, gentle voice) instinct

pusillanimity, pusillanimity (timidity and the fear of taking risks) instincts

put down, to-put-someone-down instinct

puzzle over, to-puzzle-over-something instinct

puzzled, creasing-the-forehead-when-you-are-puzzled instinct

puzzled, to-be-puzzled instinct

pyrophobia, pyrophobia (fear of fire) instinct

Q

q the-*q*-speech-sounds instinct (The *q* speech sounds are the minimal units of instinctual speech sounds that correspond roughly to the letter *q* of the alphabet)

quake, quake instinct

qualm, qualm instinct

quarrel, a-quarrel-consisting-of-an-interchange-of-insults-and-rebukes instinct

quaver, someone's-voice-quavers (sounds unsteady, uncertain and nervous) instinct

queasy, feeling-queasy instinct

queer, a-queer-feeling instinct

queer, a-queer-sensation instinct

queerness, queerness instinct

quest, quest intinct
question, question instinct
questioning, to-have-a-questioning-expression-on-one's-face instinct
questions, children's-questions instinct
quibble, to-quibble-about-something instinct
quiescence, quiescence (a feeling of restfulness) instinct
quietness, quietness instinct
quietness, quietness-of-authority instinct
quizzical, a-quizzical-expression instinct
quizzical, a-quizzical-glance instinct
quizzical, a-quizzical-look instinct
quizzical, quizzical-amusement instinct
quizzical, to-stare-quizzically instinct

R

r, the-*r*-speech-sounds instinct (The *r* speech sounds are the minimal units of instinctual speech sounds that correspond roughly to the letter *r* of the alphabet)
rabble, rabble-rousing instinct
racial, racial-consciousness instinct
racial, racial-prejudice instinct
racism, racism instinct (Remember: instincts *can* learn)
raconteur, raconteur instinct
radicalism, radicalism instinct
rage, feeling-of-rage instinct
rage, rage instinct
rage, rage-at-ego-injury instinct
rage, uncontrollable-rage instinct
rage, violent-rage instinct
raillery, raillery instinct

raise, to-raise-one's-voice instinct
raising, raising-eyebrows-in-surprise instinct
rancor, rancor instinct
rank, networks-of-rank-and-status instinct
rank, the-struggle-for-rank instinct
rapid, rapid-eye-movement (REM) instinct
rational, ordinary-rational-control instincts
rational, rational-willing instinct
rationalization, rationalization instinct
reality, reality-feeling instinct
reality, to-construct-physical-reality instincts
rearing, child-rearing instinct
reason, reason-is-the-slave-of-the-passions instincts
reasoning, reasoning instinct
reassurance, a-sense-of-reassurance instinct
reassured, to-be-reassured-by-someone instinct
rebel, to-rebel-against-parental-authority instinct
rebellious, rebellious-behavior instinct
rebellious, the-rebellious-teenage-years instinct
rebelliousness, rebelliousness instinct
rebuke, you-rebuke-someone instinct
recall, recall instincts (e.g. to-recall-facts instinct)
recall, we-are-sometimes-unable-to-recall-some-very-unpleasant-or-threat-ening-memories instinct
recklessness, recklessness instinct
reclaiming, reclaiming instinct (Natural, spontaneous behavior is instinctual behavior!)
recognition, pattern-recognition instincts
recognition, recognition instinct
recognition, the-use-of-the-face-for-personal-recognition instinct
reconciliation, reconciliation instinct
recrimination, recrimination instinct

recriminatory, recriminatory-arguments instinct

rectitude, rectitude instinct

redirected, redirected-activities instinct (actions diverted on to a bystander)

redirected, redirected-aggression instinct (sometimes the redirection process is greatly delayed in its expressions)

reflection, reflection instinct (considering instinct)

reflectively, to-scratch-one's-chin-reflectively instinct

reflex, reflex instincts. Reflexes are instincts ("little instincts"), but instincts are not necessarily reflexes. Reflexes can learn. There are an enormous number of reflexes. More than 70 infant reflexes have been identified.

reflexive, reflexive-behavior instincts (e.g. «Reflexively, he stepped backwards»)

regression, regression instinct (e.g. a 12-year-old child may show regression by thumb sucking)

regret, to-regret instinct (= regret instinct)

rejection, rejection instinct (normal behavior needs to be explained!)

rejoicing, rejoicing-behavior instinct

relationship, a-love-hate-relationship instincts

relationships, the-need-to-have-relationships-with-others instinct

relaxation, a-sense-of-relaxation instinct

relaxation, a-state-of-calm-relaxation instinct

relaxation, deep-relaxation instinct

relaxation, relaxation-feeling instinct

relaxation, the-postures-of-relaxation instincts (nightly sleep, the full sleeping pattern, dozing, the forty winks, the catnap, the snooze, the vertical lean, the arms support, the head support, the sitting down, the body slump, the lying-down, the full limbs sprawl, the one-leg stand, the knee-kneel, the double knee-kneel, the all-fours rest, the squat-kneel, the flat-footed squat, the tiptoe squat, the squat-sit, the full legs-fold posture, the lotus position, the simple leg side-curl, breaks, 'a change is as good as a rest', etc)

relaxation, the-relaxation-response instinct

release, feeling-of-release instinct

relief, comic-relief instinct

relief, feelings-of-relief instinct

relief, relief instinct

relief, to-sigh-with-relief instinct

religion, religion-affiliation instinct

religious, a-moment-of-sudden-religious-insight-or-awakening instinct

religious, religious-belief instinct

religious, religious-emotion instincts

religious, religious-trance instinct

reluctance, to-do-something-with-a-feeling-of-reluctance instinct (a-feeling-of-reluctance instinct)

REM, non-REM-dreams instincts (non-REM-dreams are ordinary instincts at work during non-REM sleep)

REM, REM-dreams instincts (REM-dreams are ordinary instincts at work during REM sleep)

REM, REM-erections instinct (= erections during REM sleep = erection instinct; see above)

remember, to-remember instinct

remembrance, remembrance instinct

reminder, reminder instinct

remonstrate, to-remonstrate instinct

remorse, feelings-of-remorse instinct

remorse, remorse instinct

repartee, repartee instinct

repentance, repentance instinct

reply, reply instinct

repression, repression instincts (Remember: instincts *can* learn)

reprisal, reprisal instinct

reproach, reproach instinct

reproduction, reproduction instinct(s) (see: Introduction)

reproductive, reproductive instincts

reproof, reproof instinct

repudiation, repudiation instinct
repugnance, repugnance instinct
reputation, reputation instinct (Think! Reputation *is* an instinct!)
reputation, to-be-concerned-to-protect-one's-personal-reputation instinct
resentment, resentment instinct
resentment, to-feel-a-twinge-of-resentment instinct
reserved, to-be-reserved instinct
resignation, resignation instinct
resist, to-resist-the-urge instinct(s)
resistance, passive-resistance instinct
resistance, resistance instinct
resistance, resistance-to-temptation instincts
resolution, resolution instinct
respect, respect-for-"rank and wealth" instinct
respect, respect-of-others instinct
respecting, respecting-a-person instinct
respond sexually, to-respond-sexually-to-hemispherical-buttocks-and-red-labia-and-hemispherical-breasts-and-red-lips instincts
responsibility, a-sense-of-moral-responsibility instinct
responsibility, diffusion-of-responsibility instincts
responsibility, our-willingness-to-ascribe-responsibility instinct
responsible, holding-responsible instinct
responsible, to-be-responsible instinct (= a-sense-of-responsibility instinct)
rest activity cycle, rest-activity-cycle instincts
restlessness, restlessness instinct
restrain, to-struggle-to-restrain-one's-natural-impulses instinct (is natural!)
retaliation, retaliation instinct
retention, retention-of-information instinct
reticence, reticence instinct
retribution, the-fear-of-retribution instinct
retroactive, retroactive-association instinct
returning, returning-a-kindness instinct

revelling, revelling instinct
revenge, revenge instinct
revenge, to-nurture-thoughts-of-revenge instinct
revenge, to-plan-revenge instinct
revenge, you-feel-a-desire-for-revenge instinct
reverence, reverence instinct
reverie, reverie instinct
revile, you-revile-someone-or-something instinct
revulsion, revulsion instinct
reward, reward-dependence instinct
reward, to-reward-someone instinct
rhetorical, rhetorical-speech instinct
rhypophobia, rhypophobia (fear of defecation—the process/defeca-
tion—the product) instincts
rhyming, rhyming instinct
rhythm, rhythm instincts
rhythms, biological-rhythms instincts
ridicule, ridicule instinct
right and wrong, the-sense-of-right-and-wrong instinct
righteousness, righteousness instinct
rigidity, rigidity instincts
riot, riot instinct
ripe language, ripe-language instinct
riposte, riposte instinct
risk taking, risk-taking instinct
ritual, ritual instinct(s) (see: Introduction)
rivalry, rivalry instinct
rivalry, sibling-rivalry instinct
rivet, people-or-things-rivet-you instinct
roar, a-roar-of-anger instinct
roasting, to-give-someone-a-roasting instinct
rock, the-infant-is-held-and-either-rocked,-patted-or-stroked instinct

rock, we-rock-back-and-forth-on-our-feet-when-we-are-in-a-state-of-conflict instinct

rock, to-rock-with-anguish instinct

rock, to-rock-with-laughter instinct

romance, romance instinct

romantic, a-romantic-fling instinct

romantic, romantic-intimacies instincts

romantic, romantic-love instinct

romantic, romantic-relationship(s) instinct

romantic, to-be-romantic instinct (romanticism instinct)

romping, romping instinct

rooting, the-rooting-reflex instinct (the rooting reflex enables the baby to take its mother's nipple in its mouth and nurse)

rote learning, rote-learning instinct

rotten, to-dread-the-odor-of-rotten-eggs,-vegetables,-etc instinct

rough, rough-and-tumble-play instinct

row, a-family-row instincts

rub, to-rub-one's-chin-thoughtfully instinct

rude, a-readiness-to-be-rude instinct

rude, rude-gesture instincts (e.g. to put one's tongue out)

rude, to-be-rude-to-people instinct (rudeness instinct)

rule, rule-worship instinct

ruling, a-ruling-idea-or-feeling instinct

rumination, quiet-sessions-of-rumination instinct

rumination, rumination instinct

rumor, rumor instinct

rumors, to-peddle-rumors instinct

run away with, a-feeling-runs-away-with-you instinct

running, running instinct

rush, a-rush-in-someone's-physical-feelings-or-emotions instincts

ruthlessness, ruthlessness instinct

S

s, the-*s*-speech-sounds instinct (The *s* speech sounds are the minimal units of instinctual speech sounds that correspond roughly to the letter *s* of the alphabet)

saccadic movement, saccadic-movement instinct

sacredness, sacredness instinct

sacrifices, to-make-sacrifices-for-something instinct

sadism, sadism instinct

sadness, sadness instinct

sadness, the-sadness-that-accompanies-a-setback instinct

safety, to-strive-for-safety-and-security instinct

saliva, the-ceasing-of-secretion-of-saliva-on-intense-excitement instinct

salivation, salivation instincts (e.g. the mere thought of food makes you start to salivate)

saltiness, to-sense-saltiness instinct

salutation, salutation instinct (we are, in general, incapable of beginning or ending any kind of encounter without performing some type of salutation)

sanctification, sanctification instinct

sanctions, penal-sanctions instinct

sanctity, the-sanctity-of-something instinct

sanguine, you-are-sanguine-about-something instinct

sarcasm, sarcasm instinct

sarcastic, sarcastic-remark instinct

sardonic, sardonic-behavior instinct

sardonic, sardonic-humor instinct (= grim-humor instinct)

satiety, the-feeling-of-satiety-after-a-meal instinct

satire, satire instinct

satisfaction, job-satisfaction instinct

satisfaction, satisfaction instinct

satisfaction, the-restful-satisfaction-from-an-altruistic-act-well-and-truly-placed instinct

satisfying, satisfying-emotional-experience instinct

savagery, savagery instinct

savor, to-savor-food-or-drink instinct

scaling, scaling-of-responses-in-aggressive-interactions instincts

scapegoating, scapegoating instinct

scolding, scolding instinct

scolding, the-scolding-charges-of-racism-and-sexism instinct (Natural, spontaneous behavior is instinctual behavior)

scar, an-unpleasant-experience-scars-one's-mind instinct

scared, the-scared-face instinct

scared, to-be-scared instinct

scene, to-make-a-scene instinct

scent, scent (a pleasant smell) instinct

scent, you-scent-something (you begin to feel that it is going to happen)

scoffing, scoffing instinct

scolding, scolding instinct

scopophilia, scopophilia (the deriving of sexual pleasure from visual sources) instinct

scopophobia, scopophobia (fear of being seen by others) instinct

scorn, laughter-of-scorn instinct

scorn, scorn instinct

scorn, to-laugh-to-scorn instinct

scotophobia, scotophobia (fear of the dark/darkness) instincts (not used for the common condition in children and adults)

scourge, you-scourge-someone instinct

scout, to-scout-the-surrounding-area instinct

scrap, to-love-a-scrap instinct

scratch, to-scratch-a-part-of-one's-body instinct

scream, to-scream instinct

scream, to-scream-in-terror instinct

screaming, screaming-child instinct
scrutinizing, scrutinizing instinct
scuffle, scuffle instinct
scuttle, to-scuttle-somewhere instinct
search, to-search-one's-mind-for-something instinct
searing, to-feel-a-searing-pain instinct
seasickness, seasickness instinct
secure, to-feel-secure instinct (= the-feeling-of-security instinct)
seditious, seditious-behavior instinct
seduce, to-charm-and-seduce-the-sex-object instinct
seduction, seduction instinct
seeing, seeing instincts
seize, to-seize-something instinct
selective, selective-attention instinct
selective, selective-inattention instinct
self, a-sense-of-self-and-other instinct
self, feeling-of-self instinct
self, negative-self-feeling instinct
self, positive-self-feeling instinct
self-abandonment, self-abandonment instinct
self-abasement, self-abasement instinct (feeling-of-inferiority instinct)
self-abnegation, self-abnegation instinct
self-absorption, self-absorption instinct
self-accusation, self-accusation instinct
self-activity, self-activity instinct
self-actualization, self-actualization instinct
self-advertisement instinct
self-assertiveness, self-assertiveness instinct
self-assurance, self-assurance instinct
self-attention, self-attention instinct
self-attribution, self-attribution instinct
self-awareness, self-awareness instinct

self-blame, self-blame instinct
self-complacency, self-complacency instinct
self-conceit, self-conceit instinct
self-conception, self-conception instinct
self-condemnation, self-condemnation instinct
self-confidence, self-confidence instinct
self-consciousness, self-consciousness instinct
self-control, self-control instinct
self-correction, self-correction instinct
self-criticism, self-criticism instinct
self-deceit, self-deceit instinct
self-deception instinct
self-defense, self-defense instincts
self-degradation, self-degradation instinct
self-denial, self-denial instinct
self-directedness, self-directedness instinct
self-discipline, self-discipline instinct
self-discovery, self-discovery instinct
self-display, self-display instinct (positive-self-impulse instinct)
self-distrust instinct
self-doubt, self-doubt instinct
self-effacing, self-effacing instinct
self-efficacy, a-sense-of-self-efficacy instinct
self-entertainment instinct
self-esteem, self-esteem instinct
self-evaluation, self-evaluation instinct
self-expression, self-expression instinct
self-grooming, self-grooming instincts
self-identity, self-identity instinct
self-image, self-image instinct
self-importance, a-sense-of-self-importance instinct
self-improvement, the-concern-with-self-improvement instinct

self-indulgence, self-indulgence instinct

self-intimacies, self-intimacies instincts (the hair clasp, the mouth touch, the temple support, the cheek support, the chin support, the jaw support, interlocking the fingers, clasping one palm with another, clasping one hand tightly in the other, the folded arms, the self-hug, leg-hugging, thigh-clasping, the touching finger tips, the head-lowered-on-to-shoulder posture, rock ourselves back and fourth, etc)

self-love, self-love instinct

self-perception, self-perception instinct

self-pity, self-pity instinct (= the-mood-of-self-pity instinct)

self-possessed, to-be-self-possessed instinct

self-preservation, self-preservation instinct(s) (see: Introduction)

self-realization, self-realization instinct

self-recognition, self-recognition instinct

self-recrimination instinct

self-renunciation instinct

self-repression instinct

self-reproach instinct

self-respect, self-respect instinct

self-restraint, self-restraint-with-respect-to-bodily-discharges instinct

self-restraint, self-restraint-with-respect-to-sexual-impulses instinct

self-righteousness, self-righteousness instinct

self-sacrifice, self-sacrifice instinct

self-satisfaction, self-satisfaction instinct

self-sentiment, self-sentiment instinct

selfish, to-be-selfish instinct

selfish, to-be-unselfish instinct

selflessness, we-universally-admire-and-praise-selflessness,-but-we-simply-do-not-practice-what-we-preach instinct

semantic, semantic-memory instinct (memory for meaning)

semantic, to-infer-semantic-meaning instinct

semismile, a-semismile-expression instinct

semiwakeful, a-semiwakeful-state instinct
sensation, sensation-seeking instinct
sensationalism, sensationalism instinct
sensitized, sensitized-hand instinct (the-sensitive-nature-of-our-hands instinct)
sensory, sensory-seeking instincts
sensual, sensual-pleasure instincts
sentences, memory-for-tacit-implications-of-sentences instinct
sentences, to-speak-in-sentences instinct
sentience, sentience need (need for sensual pleasures) instinct
sentimentality, sentimentality instinct
sentimentalizing, sentimentalizing instinct
separation, infant's-separation-anxiety instinct
separation, separation-anxiety instinct
serenity, serenity instinct
serial, serial-monogamy instinct
sermonizing, sermonizing
servility, servility instinct
seven-plus-or-minus-two, seven-plus-or-minus-two instinct (the term denotes the number of discrete pieces of information that can be held in short-term memory at one time)
sex appeal, the-feel-of-sex-appeal instinct
sex experimentation, sex-experimentation-among-children instinct
sex feeling, sex-feeling instinct
sex play in children, sex-play-in-children instinct (overt sex-play romping)
sexiness, sexiness instinct
sexual activity, sexual-activity-continuous-through-menstrual-cycle instinct
sexual advertisement, sexual-advertisement instinct
sexual arousal, sexual-arousal instinct
sexual desire, sexual-desires instinct
sexual ecstasy, sexual-ecstasy instinct
sexual excitement, sexual-excitement instinct

sexual fantasies, sexual-fantasies instinct

sexual flush, sexual-flush instinct

sexual gratification, sexual-gratification instinct

sexual identity, sexual-identity instinct

sexual intimacy, sexual-intimacy instincts

sexual jealousy, sexual-jealousy instinct

sexual masochism, sexual-masochism instinct

sexual orientation, sexual-orientation instincts

sexual passion, sexual-passion instinct

sexual pleasure, sexual-pleasure instincts

sexual response, the-sexual-response-cycle instinct

sexual restrictions, sexual-restrictions instinct

sexual sadism, sexual-sadism instinct

sexual violence, sexual-violence instinct (Remember: instincts *can* learn)

shade, to-shade-one's-eyes instinct

shaking, shaking-a-fist-at-someone instinct

shaking, the-baby-is-shaking-its-head-from-side-to-side (= no, no, no) instinct

shame, shame instinct

shamefaced, to-be-shamefaced instinct

shape, by-feeling-the-physical-thing-you-determine-its-shape instinct

share, disrespect-for-those-who-would-not-share instinct

share, to-feel-a-need-to-share-your-excitements instinct

share, to-share-an-enthusiasm-or-an-interest instinct

share, to-share-food instinct

sharp, sharp-remarks instinct

shelter, finding-shelter instinct

shiver, a-shiver-of-excitement instinct

shivering, to-be-shivering-because-you-are-cold instinct

shivering, to-be-shivering-because-you-are-frightened instinct

shock, the-need-to-shock-others instinct

shoo, to-shout-'Shoo!'-at-an-animal-in-order-to-make-it-go-away instinct

short temper, short-temper instinct
short term memory, short-term-memory instinct
shorter, men-seek-shorter-wives instinct
shoulder, to-put-an-arm-around-a-friend's-shoulder instinct
shout, to-shout instinct
shout, to-shout-encouragement-to-people instinct
shout, to-shout-something-out instinct
show, show-someone/something-off instinct
show, to-show-someone-round instinct
shriek, to-shriek-in-alarm instinct
shriek, to-shriek-with-laughter instinct
shriek, to-shriek-with-pain instinct
shriek, to-shriek-with-terror instinct
shrillness, shrillness instinct
shrug, to-shrug-one's-shoulders instinct
shudder, to-shudder instinct
shush, to-say-'shush'-when-you-are-telling-someone-to-be-quiet instinct
shy, a-shy-smile instinct
shy, to-be-too-shy-to-speak instinct
shyness, shyness instinct (Note: infants show shyness)
sickness, feelings-of-"sickness" instinct
sides, to-take-sides (with someone) instinct
sigh, to-sigh instinct
sight, the-sight-of-food-triggers-a-desire-to-eat instinct
sign language, sign-language instincts
silent, silent-emotion instinct
similarity, the-principle-of-similarity instinct (the viewer perceives similar things as being related)
simplification, simplification instinct
simulate, to-simulate-a-feeling-or-an-action instinct
sincerity, sincerity instinct
singing, singing instinct

sisterhood, sisterhood instinct

situation, to-identify-the-current-situation-as-being-of-a-certain-kind instinct

skepticism, skepticism instinct

skin, like-the-feel-of-something-on-your-skin instinct (= skin-pleasure instinct)

skin, skin-contact instinct (= body-contact instinct)

skin, skin-eroticism instinct

skin, the-naked-skin-of-the-woman-is-used-as-a-sexual-releaser instinct

skin, the-skin-sense instinct

skip, to-skip instinct

slap, you-slap-someone-on-the-back instinct

sleep, non-REM-sleep instinct

sleep, REM-sleep instinct

sleep, sleep-wake-schedule instinct

sleep, the-postures-of-sleep instincts

sleepiness, the-feeling-of-sleepiness instinct

sleepwalking, sleepwalking instinct

slight, to-slight-someone instinct

slobbering mouth, the-slobbering-mouth-of-the-intensely-inhibited-assault instinct

sloppiness, sloppiness instinct

sloth, sloth instinct

slurp, to-slurp-a-liquid instinct

sly, to-give-a-sly-gesture instinct

sly, to-give-a-sly-look instinct

sly, to-give-a-sly-remark instinct

slyness, slyness instinct

smack, to-smack-one's-lips instinct

small, small-talk instinct

smell, beautiful-women-smell-nice instinct

smell, the-emotional-and-behavioral-aspects-of-smell-sensation instincts

smell, the-sense-of-smell-contributes-to-the-sense-of-taste instinct
smell, the-smell-of-food-triggers-the-desire-to-eat instinct
smells, certain-smells-remind-you-of-certain-places instinct
smells, something-smells-pleasant/unpleasant instincts
smile, a-beaming-smile instinct
smile, a-big,-happy-smile instinct
smile, infants-smile-at-the-faces-of-their-caregivers instinct
smile, the-smile-on-the-face-of-a-fighting-boy instinct
smiles, smiles-of-admiration instinct
smiling, smiling instincts
smiling, smiling-child instinct
smiling, the-smiling-face instinct
smirk, to-smirk instinct
smugness, smugness instinct
snake, the-snake-reaction instinct
snakes, our-fascination-with-snakes instinct
snap, to-snap-at-someone instinct
snarl, the-open-mouthed-snarl instinct (the-intention-movements-of-biting instinct)
snarl, to-snarl-something instinct
sneer, sneer (the facial expression) instinct
sneer, to-sneer-at-someone-or-something instinct
snicker, to-snicker instinct
snide, a-snide-comment-or-remark instinct
snigger, to-snigger instinct
snobbery, snobbery instinct
snobbishness, snobbishness instinct
snore, snore instinct
so what, a 'so what?'-feeling instinct
sob, to-sob instinct (= sobbing instinct)
social, social instincts
social, social-bonding instinct

social, social-facilitation instinct

social, social-hierarchy instinct(s) (see: Introduction)

social, social-imitation instinct

social, social-intimacies instinct

social, social-loafing instinct

social, social-phobia instincts (= fear of social situations)

social, social-status instinct

social, social-stigma instinct

social, social-tension instincts

social, to-avoid-social-stigma instinct

social, to-calculate-social-obligations instinct

social, to-interpret-social-situations instincts

socialization, socialization instincts (perhaps most instincts are social-ization instincts)

soft, to-be-soft-hearted instinct

soft, to-get-a-sensual-pleasure-from-touching-soft-things instinct

softly, to-cry-softly instinct

solace, solace instinct

solemnity, his/her-mask-of-solemnity instinct

solemnity, the-sense-of-solemnity instinct

soliciting, soliciting-behavior instinct

solicitude, your-solicitude-for-someone instinct

solidarity, in-group-solidarity instinct

solidarity, solidarity instinct

solitude, the-terror-of-absolute-solitude instinct

solving, problem-solving-activity instincts

solving, to-enjoy-solving-problems instinct

soothing, soothing instincts (e.g. we employ stroking and patting movements to soothe an agitated individual)

soothing, soothing-a-baby-ain't-no-cure-for-the-baby-blues instinct

sore, a-sore-point instinct

sore, if-part-of-your-body-is-sore,-it-causes-you-pain-and-discomfort instinct

sore, you-are-sore-about-something instinct

soreness, a-feeling-of-body-soreness instinct

sorrow, a-feeling-of-sorrow instinct

sorry, to-be-sorry-about-a-situation instinct

sound, localization-of-sound instinct

sound, the-reflexive-turning-of-the-head-and-eyes-in-the-direction-of-a-sudden-or-alarming-sound instinct

sounds, sounds-conjure-up-memories-for-you instinct

sounds, sounds (represented by the letters of the alphabet)-in-a-language instincts

sounds, the-elementary-sounds-of-human-nonlinguistic-communication instincts

sourness, to-sense-sourness instinct

space, space-perception instincts (position,-direction,-form,-and-magnitude instincts)

space, space-time-matter instincts

spaces, dread-in,-and-of,-open-spaces instinct

spaces, dread-of-confined-spaces instinct

spank, to-spank-a-child instinct

spatial, spatial-orientation instinct

spatial, spatial-reasoning instinct

spatial, spatial-skills instincts

speciesism, speciesism instinct

speculation, speculation instinct

speculative, speculative-interpretation instinct

speech, speech-rhythm instinct

speech, to-produce-speech-sounds instincts

spider, the-spider-reaction instinct

spit, the-disgust-that-makes-you-spit-out-bad-tasting-food instinct

spit, to-spit instinct

spite, spite instinct

spontaneous friendship, spontaneous-friendship-formation instinct

spree, spree instinct

sprint, to-sprint instinct (see locomotion instincts)

squabble, family-squabble instinct

squabbling, squabbling instinct

squealing, squealing instinct

squeamishness, squeamishness instinct

squeeze, when-a-man-and-a-woman-have-to-squeeze-past-each-other,-the-man-twists-towards-the-woman,-while-she-twists-away-from-him instinct

stage fright, stage-fright instinct

stamina, stamina instinct

stamp, people-stamp-their-feet-when-they-are-angry instinct

stand, stand-with-more-weight-on-one-leg-and-stick-out-one-hip-more-than-the-other instinct

stand up fight, stand-up-fight instinct

standing, standing-your-ground instinct

stare, a-hostile-stare instinct

stare, stare-fixedly-into-space instinct

stare, to-feel-that-somebody-stare-at-you instinct

stare, to-give-somebody-a-hard-stare instinct

stare, to-stare-angrily-at-somebody instinct

staring, staring-at-interesting-visual-stimuli instinct

startle, startle-response instinct

startle, the-startle-posture instinct

stasibasiphobia, stasibasiphobia (fear of standing erect and walking) instinct

stasiphobia, stasiphobia (fear of standing) instinct

static sense, the-emotional-and-behavioral-aspects-of-the-static-sense instincts

statistics, reasoning-about-statistics instinct

status, men-demonstrate-their-prowess-in-order-to-generate-status instinct

status, status-differentiation instinct
status, status-seeking instinct
status, the-display-of-status instinct
status, to-be-conscious-of-his/her-status-among-colleagues instinct
stay, to-stay-in-love instincts (having fallen in love, he/she would have to stay in love)
stench, stench (a strong and very unpleasant smell) instinct
stereotyping, stereotyping-people instinct
stern, a-stern-look-or-expression instinct
sternness, sternness instinct
stew, to-be-in-a-stew instinct
stiff, to-keep-a-stiff-upper-lip instinct
stiffness, a-feeling-of-body-stiffness instinct
stimulus generalization, stimulus-generalization instinct
stinginess, stinginess instinct
stinginess, to-be-intolerant-of-stinginess instinct
stirred, to-be-stirred instinct
stories, we-love-to-hear-stories instinct
story, telling-a-particular-story instinct
straight, to-keep-a-straight-face instinct
strain, mental-strains instinct
strange, to-feel-a-bit-strange instinct
strangeness, to-feel-the-strangeness instinct
stranger, stranger-anxiety-reaction-of-the-baby instinct
strangers, fear-of-strangers instinct
strangers, suspicion-of-strangers instinct
stray, your-thoughts-stray instinct
strength, a-sense-of-strength instinct
stress, reactions-to-stress instincts (the-stress-response instincts)
stress, the-stress-management instincts
stress, to-be-vulnerable-to-stress instincts
stress, to-feel-stress instinct

strictness, strictness instinct

strife, strife instinct

strike, an-idea-or-thought-strikes-you instinct

strike back, to-strike-back instinct

strike on, to-strike-on-a-solution,-answer,-plan,-etc (to unexpectedly think of it) instinct

stroke, to-stroke-someone-or-something (e.g. he stroked her hair affectionately) instinct

stroll, the-stroll-is(-also)-the-gait-of-the-man-pacing-up-and-down,-deep-in-thought instinct

strong language, strong-language instinct

struggling, struggling-for-success instinct

strut, to-strut (to walk in a proud way) instinct

stubbornness, stubbornness instinct

study, to-study instinct (in the widest sense of the word "study")

subdued, subdued-feelings instinct

sublimation, the-sublimation-of-a-strong-desire-or-feeling instinct

submission, passive-submission instincts (is much the same as in other mammals: cringing, crouching, groveling, whimpering, verbal pleading and begging for mercy, attempts to protect the most vulnerable parts of the body, etc)

subordination, subordination instincts (e.g. a subordinate (male or female) adopts a attitude of "femininity" towards a dominant individual)

subservience, subservience instinct

substitutes, our-tendency-towards-accepting-symbolic-substitutes-for-the-real-thing instinct

succeed, to-want-to-succeed instinct

success, enjoying-success instinct

success, fear-of-success instinct

success, striving-for-success instinct

sucking, sucking instinct

suckle, a-mother-suckles-a-baby instinct

sudden, sudden-body-movement instinct
suffer, to-suffer-pain-in-one's-body instinct
suffer, to-suffer-pain-in-one's-mind instinct
suffering, dread-of-suffering-or-disease instinct
sugary, to-prefer-sugary-foods instinct
suggestibility, suggestibility instinct
sullenness, sullenness instinct
sum people up, sum-people-up-after-a-first-meeting instinct
summon, to-summon-all-the-"will power" instinct
sunbathe, a-strong-tendency-to-sunbathe instinct
superior, feeling-superior instinct (= feelings-of-superiority instinct)
supernatural, beliefs-about-the-supernatural instinct
superstition, superstition instinct (superstition is a form of protective response unique to man)
supplication, supplication instinct
support, social-support instinct
support, the-need-of-a-sympathizing-support,-or-of-objects-of-admiration-and-reverence instinct
supportiveness, supportiveness instinct
suppressing, suppressing-thoughts instinct
suppression, a-deliberate-suppression-of-personal-feelings,-or-personal-likes-and-dislikes instincts
suppression, suppression instinct
sure, to-be-sure-about-one's-feelings,-wishes,-or-intentions instincts
sure, to-feel-sure instinct
surmise, you-surmise-that-something-is-true instinct
surprise, raising-eyebrows-in-surprise instinct
surprise, surprise instinct
surreptitious, surreptitious-behavior (e.g. he looked surreptitiously at his watch) instinct
survey, locality-survey instinct
survival, survival instincts («all» instincts are survival instincts)

survivor guilt, survivor-guilt instinct

suspicion, suspicion instinct

suspiciousness, suspiciousness instinct

suss, to-suss-someone-out (to discover what their true character is) instinct

swagger, to-swagger instinct

swanking, someone-is-swanking instinct

swear, to-swear instinct

sweet, a-strong-positive-response-to-sweet-tasting-objects instinct

sweet, a-sweet-smell-is-pleasant instinct

sweet, a-sweet-sound-is-pleasant instinct

sweet, to-eat-sweet-things-purely-for-pleasure instinct

sweetness, the-sweetness-of-freedom instinct

sweetness, to-sense-sweetness instinct

swim, babies-can-swim-when-only-a-few-weeks-old instinct

symbol, an-object-can-be-understood-both-as-a-thing-itself-and-as-a-symbol-of-something-else instinct

symbolophobia, symbolophobia (fear of symbols/symbolic representations) instincts

sympathy, sympathy instinct

synchrony, synchrony-of-movement-between-two-or-more-persons instinct

syncretism, syncretism instinct

synesthesia, synesthesia instincts (synesthesia is an involuntary joining in which the real information from one sense is joined or accompanies a perception in another)

syntax, syntax (the grammatical arrangement of words) instinct

T

t, the-*t*-speech-sounds instinct (The *t* speech sounds are the minimal units of instinctual speech sounds that correspond roughly to the letter *t* of the alphabet)

tact, tact-and-sensibility instinct

tactical, tactical-deception instinct

tactile, the-emotional-and-behavioral-aspects-of-the-tactile-sensations instincts

tactile, the-tactile-sensation-experienced-in-the-skin-when-a-hair-is-touched-or-moved instinct

take risks, take-risks instincts

taking, taking-sides instinct

talkativeness, talkativeness instinct

talking, exploratory-talking instinct

talking, play-talking instinct

talking. "talking back" instinct

tampering, tampering instinct

tantrum, tantrum instinct

tantrum, temper-tantrum instinct

tap, we-tap-our-feet-or-fingers-in-time-to-music instinct

taphephobia, taphephobia (fear of graves/being buried alive) instincts (also called taphophobia)

taphophobia, taphophobia (fear of graves/being buried alive) instincts (also called taphephobia)

taste, taste-sensations (sweet, sour, salty, bitter, umani) instincts (the proportions of the five basic tastes contained in the food give the food its basic flavor)

tastes, sexual-tastes instinct (Note: instincts are situational, and instincts can learn)

tasting, to-enjoy-tasting-food instinct

taunt, you-taunt-someone instinct

teaching, teaching instinct (teaching is a method of learning)

team, team-play instinct

team, team-spirit instinct

tears, the-bursting-into-tears-for-bodily-pain instinct

tears, the-bursting-into-tears-for-joy instinct

tears, the-bursting-into-tears-for-sorrow instinct

tears, to-burst-into-tears instinct

teasing, teasing instinct

teeth, to-grit-one's-teeth-with-anger instinct

telepathy, telepathy instinct

tell off, to-tell-someone-off instinct

temper, temper instinct (inborn versions: a quick temper, a violent temper, a mild temper, etc)

temper, temper-tantrum instinct

temper, to-lose-your-temper instinct

temperature, the-emotional-and-behavioral-aspects-of-the-temperature-sensations instinct

temperature, the-feeling-of-temperature-across-the-entire-skin-surface instinct

tempo, personal-tempo instinct

temptation, giving-in-to-temptation instincts (or rather the effect of instincts?)

temptation, temptation instincts (or rather the effect of instincts?)

temptation, to-resist-temptation instincts (or rather the effect of instincts?)

tenacity, tenacity instinct

tender, tender-feelings instinct

tender, you-are-tender-hearted instinct

tenderness, feeling-of-tenderness instinct

tense expectancy, tense-expectancy instinct

tenseness, tenseness instinct

tenseness, to-feel-a-tenseness instinct

tension, nervous-tension instinct

tension, tension instincts

territorial, territorial instinct(s) (see: Introduction)

territorial, territorial-behavior instinct

territorial, territorial-spacing instinct

territorial, the-territorial-imperative instinct

territoriality, territoriality instinct(s) (= territorial instinct(s))

territory, to-protect-your-territory instinct (= territorial-defense instinct)

terror, a-feeling-of-terror instinct

terror, terror (extreme degree of fear) instinct

thalassophobia, thalassophobia (fear of the sea) instinct

thanatophobia, thanatophobia (fear of death/dead things, especially human corpses) instincts

thank, to-thank instinct

thankfulness, thankfulness instinct

theatrical, theatrical-behavior instinct

theophobia, theophobia (fear of God/retribution from God for one's sins) instincts

theorizing, theorizing instinct

things, enjoying-things instincts

things, possessiveness-about-things instinct

things, the-desire-to-attain-things instinct

thinking, abstract-thinking-style instincts

thinking, concrete-operational-thinking instincts

thinking, concrete-thinking-style instincts

thinking, formal-operational-thinking instincts

thinking, thinking instincts

thirst, thirst instinct

thoughtfulness, thoughtfulness instinct

threat displays, the-facial-expressions-of-threat-displays instincts

threat gesture, threat-gesture instincts (the raised-fist threat, the stiff forefinger threat, an attack is performed in mid-air, a man can puff up his chest and draw himself up to his full height, obscene signals used as threatening devices, etc)

threat, postures-of-threat instincts

threat, the-threat-face instinct

threat, the-threat-of-punishment instinct

threat, the-threat-stare instinct

threat, threat-of-death instinct (Note: instincts are situational, and instincts can learn)

threat, vocal-threat instincts

threaten, to-threaten-away-rivals instinct

threatening, threatening-someone/something instinct

three-dimensional objects, the-innate-knowledge-about-three-dimensional-objects instincts (e.g. a baby doesn't have to learn that a picture of a dog in a book is the same kind of object as a real dog)

three dimensional vision, the-emotional-and-behavioral-aspects-of-three-dimensional-vision instincts

thrift, thrift instinct

thrill, the-thrill-of-the-chase instinct

thrilled, to-be-thrilled instinct

thrills, seeking-thrills instinct

throwing, throwing instinct

thumb, thumb-sucking instinct

thunder and lightning, the-normal-dread-of-thunder-and-lightning instinct

tickling, tickling instinct

tidiness, your-concern-with-tidiness-and-punctuality instinct

tie sign, tie-sign-reading instincts

tie-signs, body-contact-tie-signs instincts (the kiss, the hand-in-hand, the arm link, the pat, the hand shake, the shoulder embrace, the full embrace, the waist embrace, the body support, the body-guide, the caress, the hand-to-head, the head-to-head, the mock-attack, body proximity, etc)

tight lipped, the-tight-lipped-threat-glare instinct

timbre, timbre instinct (noises have their timbre, from which we may infer what is going on)

time, time-sense instincts (innately-given-knowledge-of-time instincts) The brain has many timing skills: mechanism for measuring short time intervals in the seconds to minutes range, perception of the passing of hours, days, weeks and years, etc)

timidity, timidity instinct

tingling, to-feel-tingling-in-one's-limbs instinct
tirade, tirade instinct
tiredness, feelings-of-tiredness-and-drowsiness instinct
titter, to-titter instinct
tittle tattle, tittle-tattle instinct
toddle, a-child-toddles instinct
togetherness, the-feeling-of-female-togetherness instinct
togetherness, the-feeling-of-male-togetherness instinct
tolerance, patient-tolerance instinct
tolerance, tolerance-of-pain instinct
tolerant, to-be-tolerant/intolerant instincts (= tolerance/intolerance instincts)
tomfoolery, tomfoolery instinct
tongue, the-tip-of-the-tongue-phenomenon instinct
tool, to-perceive-a-suitable-design-of-tool-for-a-certain-job instincts
tool, tool-making instincts
tool, tool-using instincts
torment, to-torment-someone instinct (Note: instincts are situational, and instincts can learn)
torment, torment instinct
touch, the-emotional-and-behavioral-aspects-of-the-touch-sensations instincts
touch, the-sense-of-touch (pressure) instinct
touch, to-be-pleasant/unpleasant-to-the-touch instincts
touch, to-reach-out-gently-to-touch-someone-in-reassurance instinct
touched, to-be-emotionally-touched-by-something instinct
touching, touching instinct
toughness, toughness instinct ("it is important to be tough")
toxophobia, toxophobia (fear of poisons/being poisoned) instincts
traditions, to-pass-on-traditions instinct
train, a-train-of-thoughts instinct

training, training (learning the skills that you need for a particular activity) instincts

trance, trance instinct

transvestism, transvestism instinct (an "abnormal" gender-identity instinct)

travel sickness, travel-sickness instinct

tremophobia, tremophobia (fear of trembling) instinct

trepidation, trepidation instinct

trial and error, to-do-something-by-trial-and-error instinct

tribal territory, tribal-territory instinct

tribalism, tribalism instinct

trichopathophobia, trichopathophobia (in women, fear of facial hair) instinct

trichophobia, trichophobia (fear of hair) instinct

trifle, you-trifle-with-someone-or-something instinct

trill, a-trilling-laugh instinct

triskaidekaphobia, triskaidekaphobia (fear of the number that results from the operation of subtracting 1 from 14) instinct

triumph, a-feeling-of-triumph instinct

triumph, a-note-of-triumph-in-his-voice instinct

triumph, punching-the-air-or-throwing-up-their-hands-in-triumph instinct

trophy, trophy instinct

troubled, a-troubled-facial-expression instinct

troubled, to-be-troubled instinct

trust, basic-feeling-of-trust/distrust instincts

trusting, trusting/distrusting-people instincts

truth, disregard-for-truth instinct

truth, love-of-truth instinct

try, to-try instinct (= trying instinct)

tumble, rough-and-tumble-play instinct

turn, to-turn-his/her-eyes-in-our-direction-and-check-us-out instinct

type, "She's/he's my type" instinct

U

u, the-*u*-speech-sounds instinct (The *u* speech sounds are the minimal units of instinctual speech sounds that correspond roughly to the letter *u* of the alphabet)

um, um (a sound that people make when they are hesitating) instinct

umbrage, to-take-umbrage instinct

unappetizing, unappetizing-food instinct

uncertainty, a-feeling-of-uncertainty instinct

uncomfortable, to-feel-uncomfortable instinct

unconscious sight, unconscious-sight-is-more-accurate-than-conscious-sight instinct

unconsidered, unconsidered-thoughts-and-actions instinct

uncooperativeness, uncooperativeness instinct (instincts are situational!)

unctuous, to-be-unctuous instinct

undertone, to-say-something-in-an-undertone instinct

undying love, undying-love instinct

unease, a-feeling-of-unease instinct

unfair, to-be-upset-by-unfair-behavior instinct

unfocused, someone's-eyes-are-unfocused (they are open, but not looking at-anything) instinct

unfriendly, the-unfriendly-face (curling down the mouth corners) instinct

unfriendly, to-be-unfriendly instinct

unhappiness, unhappiness instinct

unified, we(most of us)-wish-to-have-unified-attitudes-as-well-as-unified-beliefs instinct

uninhibited, to-be-uninhibited (used showing approval) instinct

unity, to-feel-a-sense-of-unity-with-the-world(universe) instinct

universal grammar, universal-grammar instinct

unkind, to-be-unkind instinct

unmusical sounds, unmusical-sounds-are-unpleasant-to-listen-to instinct

unpalatable, unpalatable-food instinct
unpleasant, unpleasant-feeling instinct
unreality, feeling-of-unreality instinct
unrest, to-feel-a-sense-of-unrest instinct
unroll, a-series-of-events-unroll-in-one's-memory instinct
unselfishness, unselfishness instinct
unsympathetic, to-be-unsympathetic instinct
unwillingness, unwillingness instinct
upset, to-be-upset-by-unfair-behavior instinct
upset, to-get/be-upset instinct
upset, to-intend-to-upset-people instinct
us, the-feelings-of-"us"-versus-"them" instinct
used, to-get-used-to-something-or-someone instinct

V

v, the-*v*-speech-sounds instinct (The *v* speech sounds are the minimal units of instinctual speech sounds that correspond roughly to the letter *v* of the alphabet)
vacant, a-vacant-look-or-expression instinct
vaginal, vaginal-lubrication instinct
vain, to-be-vain instinct
vainglorious, vainglorious-behavior instinct
valor, valor (great bravery in battle) instinct
vanity, vanity instinct
vehemence, vehemence instinct
veiled, a-veiled-expression-on-one's-face instinct
venerate, you-venerate-someone instinct (= veneration instinct)
veneration, a-sentiment-of-veneration instinct
vengeance, vengeance instinct
vengeful, vengeful-pleasure instinct

vengefulness, vengefulness instinct (= you-are-vengeful instinct)

venturesome, a-venturesome-spirit instinct

veracity, veracity instinct

verbal, verbal-communication(language) instincts (= the utterance of words and sentences)

verbal, verbal-violence instinct

versions, our-ability-to-imagine-different-versions-of-events instinct

vertigo, vertigo instinct

vexed, a-vexed-frown instinct

vexed, to-be-vexed instinct

vibrancy, vibrancy instinct

vibrant, a-vibrant-voice instinct

vibration sensations, the-emotional-and-behavioral-aspects-of-vibration-sensations instincts

vice, hating-vice instinct

vicious, vicious-language instinct

victimize, to-victimize-someone-because-you-do-not-like-their-beliefs instinct

victory, victory-celebration instinct

views, to-get-angry-if-people-do-not-agree-with-your-political-or-religious-views instinct

vigilance, vigilance instinct

vigilante, a-vigilante-group instinct

vigorated, to-feel-vigorated instinct

vileness, vileness instinct

vindictiveness, vindictiveness instinct

violence, physical-violence instinct

violent, men-are-more-violent-than-women instinct

violent, preparing-the-body-for-violent-activity instincts

violent, violent-behavior instinct

violent, violent-rage instinct

virtue, loving-virtue instincts

virulence, virulence instinct

visceral, visceral-sensation instinct

vision, vision (a mental picture) instinct

visiting, visiting instinct (normal behavior needs to be explained!)

visual, visual-awareness instinct

visual, visual-grasp-reflex instinct

visual, visual-illusions instincts

visual, visual-imagery instinct

visual, visual-sensation-and-perception instincts

visualization, visualization instinct

vitriol, vitriol instinct

vocal, vocal-paralanguage instincts (grunts, giggles, laughs, sobs, cries, etc)

vocal, vocal-stress-in-a-spoken-sentence instinct

vocational, vocational-interests instincts (= vocation instincts)

voice, neutral-voice instinct

voice, people-rely-on-facial-expression-and-tone-of-voice-to-judge-a-person's-emotional-state instincts

voice, to-raise-one's-voice instinct

voice, tone-of-voice instincts

voice, voice instincts (see examples above)

void, an-aching-void-in-one's-heart instinct

volition, volition instinct

vomiting, the-emotional-and-behavioral-aspects-of-vomiting instinct

vow, you-vow-to-do-something instinct (normal behavior needs to be explained!)

voyeurism, voyeurism instinct

vulgar, to-scream-vulgar-insults instinct

vulgar, vulgar-gestures instinct

vulgar, vulgar-insults instinct

vulgar, vulgar-remarks instinct

vulnerability, vulnerability instincts (many instincts are vulnerable)

vulnerable, vulnerable-to-stress-and-pressure instincts (many instincts are vulnerable)

W

w, the-*w*-speech-sounds instinct (The *w* speech sounds are the minimal units of instinctual speech sounds that correspond roughly to the letter *w* of the alphabet)

wail, to-wail instinct

waist, men-everywhere-find-women-with-a-waist-to-hip-ratio-of-0.7-sexually-alluring instinct

waiting, waiting instinct (instincts are situational, and instincts *can* learn!)

wake, the-sleep-wake-schedule instinct

waking, waking-up instinct

wander, one's-thoughts-wander instinct

wander, to-let-the-mind-wander,-or-go-blank,-while-continuing-to-nod-and-smile-automatically instinct

wandering, wandering,-unguided-conversations instinct

wandering, your-mind-is-wandering instincts

wanderlust, wanderlust instinct

want, want-to-succeed instinct

wanting, wanting instincts

wanton, senseless-and-wanton-cruelty instinct

wanton, wanton-aggression instinct

wanton, wanton-violence instinct

warfare, intertribal-warfare instinct (Remember: war is *not* inevitable, but as long as people dream about *violent* revolutions – leftist or rightist, then …and…and…and…)

warlike, warlike-behavior instinct

warm, to-be-warm-hearted instinct

warm, to-feel-warm instinct

warm, warm-thoughts instinct

warmth, the-emotionally-and-behavioral-aspects-of-warmth-sensations instincts

warning, warning instinct

wary, you-are-wary-about-something instinct

washing, washing-with-water instinct

watch, to-watch-for-signs-of-posible-danger-and-compare-current-infor-mation-with-information-stored-in-memory instinct

watching, to-enjoy-watching-someone/something instinct

water, to-like-cold-drinking-water-better-than-warm-drinking-water instinct

wave, to-wave-one's-hand (e.g. to wave for silence) instincts

weakness, to-feel-weakness-in-one's-limbs instinct

weariness, weariness instinct

weep, weep-(copiously-)when-emotionally-disturbed instinct

welcome, to-welcome-someone instinct

welfare, to-care-about-the-welfare-of-others instinct

well-being, the-feeling-of-well-being instinct (= the-sense-of-well-being instinct)

wetness, the-emotional-and-behavioral-aspects-of-wetness-sensations instincts

wetness, to-sense-wetness instinct

whacked, to-be-whacked instinct

wheedling, helpless-little-girl-actions-as-part-of-a-wheedling-process instinct

wheedling, wheedling-persuasion instinct

whim, "his/her tendency to change his/her mind at whim" instincts

whimper, to-whimper instinct

whims, momentary-whims instincts

whining, the-child's-whining instinct

whining, whining instinct (= someone-whines-about-something instinct)

whisper, to-whisper instinct

white lie, white-lie instinct

whole, to-want-to-understand-a-thousand-"little things"-to-make-a-great-whole instinct

whoop, to-whoop-with-delight instinct

whoops, people-say-'Whoops!'-when-they-have-a-slight-accident-or-see-someone-else-having-one instinct

wild, to-be-wild-with-excitement instinct

wild, to-have-wild-eyes (a wild look) instinct

will, feeling-free-will-exist instinct (the-intuitive-belief-in-free-will instinct)

will, feeling-of-will instinct

win, like-to-win instinct

wince, to-wince instinct (= wincing instinct)

wind, to-wind-someone-up instinct

wink, to-wink-at-someone instinct

wishful thinking, wishful-thinking instinct

wishing, wishing instincts

wistfulness, wistfulness instinct

wit, wit-in-speech instinct

witty, a-witty-remark-or-joke instinct

witty, to-be-witty instinct

woe, woe instinct

wonder, a-feeling-of-wonder instinct

wonder, the-extreme-sense-of-wonder-which-we-all-feel-when-confronted-with-highly-complicated-machinery instinct

work, a-desire-to-understand-how-things-work instinct

working, working-memory instinct

worry, worry instincts

worry, worry-about-looking-foolish instinct

worry, worry-about-the-safety-of-relatives-and-close-friends instinct

worry, worry-about-what-other-people-think-about-you instinct

worship, hero-worship instinct

worship, to-worship-our-gods instinct

worship, worship instincts
worship, worship-of-authority instinct
wow, you-say-'Wow!'-when-you-are-very-impressed-by-something-or-very-pleased-about-something instinct
wrath, wrath instinct
wrestling, good-natured-wrestling-among-the-boys instinct
wretchedness, a-feeling-of-wretchedness instinct
wry, a-wry-smile instinct

X

x, the-*x*-speech-sounds instinct (The *x* speech sounds are the minimal units of instinctual speech sounds that correspond roughly to the letter *x* of the alphabet)
xenophobia, xenophobia (fear of strangers) instinct (both humans and animals show xenophobic behavior)
xenophobic, our-propensity-for-xenophobic-killing-of-other-human-groups instinct

Y

y, the-*y*-speech-sounds instinct (The *y* speech sounds are the minimal units of instinctual speech sounds that correspond roughly to the letter *y* of the alphabet)
yammer, to-yammer instinct
yarn, someone-spins-you-a-yarn (they tell you a story which is not true, (often) as an excuse for something) instinct
yawning, yawning instinct
yawning, yawning-(really-)is-infectious instinct
yearn, to-yearn-for-something instinct
yell, babies-yell-when-they-are-being-fed-too-little instinct

yelp, a-flinching,-lurching,-terrified-yelp instinct
yelp, a-yelp-of-pain instinct
yes, the-head-nod-for-'yes' instinct
youthful, youthful-rebellion instinct

Z

z, the-*z*-speech-sounds instinct (The *z* speech sounds are the minimal units of instinctual speech sounds that correspond roughly to the letter *z* of the alphabet)
zealous, to-be-zealous instinct
zest, the-zest-of-flavors instinct
zest, zest instinct
zonked, to-feel-zonked instinct

ABOUT THE AUTHOR

This dictionary is probably the first dictionary of human instincts to be published. Moreover, the Introduction of the dictionary contains the first publication of the new and important *Bronston heritability coefficient*.

Nils K. Oeijord was born in Norway in 1947. A graduate of the Agricultural University of Norway, he also studied mathematics at the University of Trondheim, in Norway as well. He is a former assistant professor of mathematics at Tromsoe College, Norway, and is the author of several scientific works in Norwegian. He is currently a full time science writer. Nils K. Oeijord's first book in English, *Human Instincts Explained*, was published in 2000 (Vantage, New York).

Mitch Bronston was born in Sioux City, Iowa and is 52 years old. He is a graduate of Drake University, and currently a science writer and facilitator of abnormal human behavior. His recent papers on *Primal Instincts and Their Effect on Human Behavior* appear widely on science websites. Previously, he has taught neuro-electrophysiology at a St Louis technical school, and now lives in Sioux City. Mitch and his wife Sydney have four grown children.

Note: *A Dictionary of Human Instincts* also appears as an appendix to *Human Behavior: The New Synthesis* by Mitch Bronston and Nils K. Oeijord